The Study of
Prehistoric Change

THE STUDY OF PREHISTORIC CHANGE

FRED T. PLOG

Department of Anthropology
State University of New York at Binghamton
Binghamton, New York

ACADEMIC PRESS   New York and London

A Subsidiary of Harcourt Brace Jovanovich, Publishers

ACADEMIC PRESS, INC.
111 Fifth Avenue, New York, New York 10003

United Kingdom Edition published by
ACADEMIC PRESS, INC. (LONDON) LTD.
24/28 Oval Road, London NW1

Library of Congress Cataloging in Publication Data

Plog, Fred. T.
    The study of prehistoric change.

    (Studies in archeology series)
    Bibliography: p.
    1.   Indians of North America—Southwest, New—
Antiquities.   2.   Archeology—Methodology.   3.   Social
change.   4.   Southwest, New—Antiquities.   I.   Title.
E78.S7P55   970.4'9   73-17114
ISBN 0–12–785645–5

Contents

Preface

This book is an exploration of two topics: the nature of cultural and behavioral change as reflected in the archeological record and the nature of prehistoric social organization.

I am convinced that what archeologists have to offer as social scientists is an understanding of long-term change. For me, the archeological record is a record of change. It holds limited potential for the understanding of the structure and functioning of societies in a synchronic frame. I am equally convinced that in our efforts to understand change, we are largely on our own. Models borrowed from sister disciplines whose data and questions differ so substantially from our own can be of only limited utility in understanding change. Our characteristic borrowing of these models has typically hindered rather than helped our efforts to understand change. While I, too, have borrowed models, they are largely taken from a particular social science tradition that is directly concerned with the study of change: the literature of economic development.

I am equally convinced that efforts to understand prehistoric social organization are likely to go astray when archeologists begin to employ the familiar terms of the ethnographer—matrilineality, matrilocality, tribe, band, etc. Our data are artifacts. One can indeed ask questions about artifacts that inform the questioner about prehistoric social organization. But, these are questions about artifacts and the distribution of artifacts—the number and number of kinds of artifacts found at discrete spatial and temporal loci—not questions about behavioral norms that may or may not be accurately reflected in the archeological record. I try to identify in this book questions about artifacts and their distributions and concomitant organizational phenomena.

While many of the issues upon which this research focuses are ones identified with the "new archeology," many are not. My departures from the philosophical and theoretical traditions associated with new archeology are made in honest disagreement with these traditions and not in a misunderstanding of them. I should, of course, be held responsible for the successes and failures of such departures.

The shortcomings of the research are undeniable. The method is not as rigorous as I consider ideal, nor are the explanations as thorough. Had I chosen a simpler problem, these deficiencies might have been remedied. But, rigorous methods and rigorous explanations are sterile companions in the absence of an interesting problem. The research is very much a compromise between what is possible and what is desirable, and it suggests somewhat more than it delivers. I can only emphasize my own intention to remedy these deficiencies in research that I carry out in the years ahead.

Acknowledgments

Many individuals have contributed to this research and the point of view that I have taken in it. I wish to thank all of those mentioned below.

Much of the research was carried on at the Field Museum of Natural History and its research station in Vernon, Arizona. Paul S. Martin gave me the opportunity to work in both these situations. Moreover, by his own scientific suggestions concerning my work and by creating an intellectual atmosphere that stimulates innovative research in anthropology, he has contributed more than any other individual to the ideas that I have expressed in this book.

John M. Fritz and Mark P. Leone were always willing to discuss at length many of the ideas that are now basic to the book.

Chris White and Ezra Zubrow assisted me in the collection of data upon which this research is based. Marcia Zubrow supervised laboratory work in the field. At the Field Museum, Christine Brightenback, Tom Cook, Wendy Farber, and Helen Pfeiffer provided willing assistance in the tiring task of analyzing and classifying specimens. Pollen and floral remains were analyzed by Dr. Richard Hevly of Northern Arizona University and Dr. Vorsila Bohrer of Boston University. Mrs. Sophie Zonas classified the faunal materials.

The undergraduate participants in the Field Museum's Undergraduate Research Participation Program performed some of the specific analyses reported herein and provided more stimulus to the direction that the research ultimately took than they probably realized. Walter Bargen, David Burkenroad, Rosalind Duncan, Mary McCutcheon, Steve Plog, Michael Schiffer, Larry Straus, Joe Traugott, Charles

Vanasse, Tom Zanic, and John Zilen played particularly important roles in this regard.

The Expedition's research was carried out under the National Science Foundation Research Grants GS 984 and GS 1919. Undergraduate participants at Vernon were supported by the National Science Foundation's Undergraduate Research Participation Program, Grant GY 2904. E. Leland Webber, the Director of the Field Museum, has also provided support for the Expedition. My graduate work at the University of Chicago was under a National Science Foundation traineeship.

Many of the ideas expressed in the worked were developed in courses with Pedro Armillas, Robert McC. Adams, and Leslie Freeman. Robert McC. Adams, Lewis Binford, Sally Binford, Glen De Garmo, Rosalind Duncan, James Hill, William Longacre, Michael Schiffer, and Stuart Struever read all, or parts of, the manuscript and made suggestions that I found valuable.

My wife, Gayle, has always been willing to lend a hand when I needed editorial and analytical assistance. Without her encouragement and cooperation, this research would have been much less productive and far less enjoyable.

CHAPTER ONE

Archeological Goals

Archeologists pursue diverse goals; we claim the ability to relate pre-history to anthropology, to social science, and to problems of the con-temporary world. But, our statements are regarded with more than mild skepticism by our anthropological colleagues. And, this skepticism is not unwarranted, for we rarely undertake research concerned with our lofty predictions of what we can do.

In fact, discussions of archeological goals appear in contexts that suggest they are not to be taken seriously. Such discussions occur at the beginning or end of works on method and theory and are largely unrelated to them. Two examples should make this point clear.

Willey and Phillips (1958:2) argue that ". . . American arch-aeology is anthropology or it is nothing." The ultimate purpose of archeology is ". . . the discovery of regularities that are in a sense spaceless and timeless." Willey and Phillips recognize, however, that archeology has made no contribution to discovering these regular-ities. "So little work has been done in American archaeology on the explanatory level that it is difficult to find a name for it [1958:5]." From these statements one would expect the remainder of their book might attempt to remedy this deficiency, but it does not. The book is,

1

instead, an extended definition and discussion of archeological units and an attempt to pigeonhole data using these units. The book is about explanation, Willey and Phillips argue, because the primary reason for our failure to explain is our failure to describe well.

Willey and Phillips have assumed good explanation results from good description of data. Such a position is methodologically un-supportable. Thorough explanations may require rigorous data collection, but the former do not necessarily result from the latter. Thorough explanations result from research that pays heed to rigor-ous standards of explanation. One hopes that archeological research is rigorous in data collection, analysis, and explanation. But, the attain-ment of rigorous standards in one of these activities does not guarantee success in the others.

K. C. Chang's *Rethinking Archaeology* also fails to relate goals and day-to-day research activities. Chang (1967a:156) sees archeology as a discipline that,

> . . . demonstrates and drives home the notion of universal values: biological urges, hate, fear, love, and brotherhood of mankind; anxiety and insatiable desire for more and better; aesthetic quality; laughter and many more. . . .
> . . .it is the archaeologist's task to present the forms and fates of past choices as objectively as he can so that in making decisions for the future the society will have the lessons of the past.

As with Willey and Phillips' work, Chang's book has little or no rela-tion to these goals; it is about classification and typology. Chang does not demonstrate that good classification will result in the attainment of his goals.

Chang (1967a:71) states that ". . . 80 or 90 percent of an archaeologist's time and energy is spent in classifying his material, the remaining 10 or 20 percent being consumed in doing something in-telligent and useful with the resultant categories." It would be a mis-take to believe that Chang is describing anything more than archeology as he sees it. Archeology does not have to be primarily classification–it is and will be what archeologists decide to make it. If in the present it is primarily classification, it need not be so in the future. But, if it is to be more than classification, archeologists must not only talk about explanation and contemporary problems, we must develop research techniques compatible with them. In so doing, we must realize that the goals, techniques of investigation, and data collection are not inde-pendent variables, but are in a dependent relationship with each other. We will not succeed in achieving one goal when our techniques of investigation are attuned to another. We will not succeed in achieving one goal even with consistent techniques of inquiry if the data we collect are attuned to a different goal. In the absence of harmony among the three goals none will be met; techniques of inquiry lacking in rigor and data collection will more probably effect chaos than a clear understanding of prehistoric phenomena.

Neither Willey and Phillips nor Chang describes a set of problems and procedures that follow from their goals. They assume that this relationship is implicit in the ways archeologists have always done things. Such, unfortunately, is not the case.

Archeological Anomie

Goals, techniques of inquiry, and data collection are dependent upon each other. That the three are interrelated does not mean there is no choice in directing research activities. It means the opposite. It means that we must define our goals, then choose techniques of inquiry and data collection that will result in meeting them.

If we were studying the occurrence of fire, no single set of self-evident variables should necessarily be used in explaining the phenomenon. It might be explained by referring to the behavior of human beings, to chemicals, to physical properties of atomic particles, or to as yet undiscovered particles of matter. Thus, many sets of data might be collected and many potential explanations might be offered for fire.

But there is no such arbitrariness in determining which variables suit a given group of investigators. A physicist will not be interested in the stimuli that cause a given man to strike a given match to set a given fire. Nor will an anthropologist be interested in the physical laws that make possible the creation of fire. Scholars select variables and explanations for phenomena on the basis of their intellectual training and the concerns of their discipline.

Archeology studies a particular set of phenomena: material objects produced by now-dead hominids. These material remains are studied in terms of a variety of potential variables. They were once explained as the result of the action of nature, God, or dwarfs. Today we deal with prehistoric phenomena in terms of a far more sophisticated, but no less bewildering, set of variables. A given artifact may be studied in terms of its raw materials, its technology of production, its technology of use, its origin as an indigenous or diffused idea, its concurrence in time and space with other artifacts, etc.

That archeologists have found so great a number of potential explanations for the occurrence of an artifact is a source of great strength to the discipline. That all these explanations have been regarded as of more or less equal merit is a source of weakness. Fifteen years ago, Spaulding (1953:590) warned against an archeology in which ". . . the only purpose of archaeology is to make archaeologists happy." One would expect this statement might have provoked an explicit discussion of goals. It did not. In a recent publication, Clarke (1968:xiii) again pointed to the multiplicity of goals archeologists pursue and found that

> Archeology is an undisciplined empirical discipline. A discipline lacking a scheme of systematic and ordered study based upon declared and clearly defined models and rules of procedure. It further lacks a body of central theory capable of synthesizing the general regularities within its data in such a way that the unique residuals distinguishing each particular case might be quickly isolated and easily assessed. . . . Lacking an explicit theory defining these entities and their relationships and transformations in a viable form, archaeology has remained an intuitive skill—an inexplicit manipulative dexterity learned by rote.

A primary reason for the image of archeologists as adventurers, fortune hunters, and curious antiquarians is our failure to develop a dialogue concerning the sorts of explanations we ought to attempt for the phenomena we study. We have no well-defined goals. There is no reason archeologists cannot be experts who happen to use prehistoric data in the explanation of cultural phenomena; but we have instead become experts in prehistoric data who attempt to tie data to cultural phenomena. A science without goals is a science warranting little intellectual respect, and at the moment, archeology is without goals.

I want to discuss what are, to me, some appropriate goals for archeologists to pursue, making an explicit assumption—that we are social scientists first, anthropologists second, and archeologists third and last. Archeology is a science that uses data from the past to test hypotheses concerning past cultural processes. A discipline that recovers data from the past and attempts to do something with it is antiquarianism, not archeology.

In this view, archeology seeks to explicate and explain prehistory. But, more than this, it attempts to use its knowledge of prehistory to contribute to anthropology, to social science, and to the understanding of human behavior. Given this view, it is possible to define explicit criteria for evaluating goals archeologists have pursued and ones we could pursue.

Criteria for Evaluating Archeological Goals

The assumptions made about the nature of archeology point to criteria by which archeological goals can be evaluated. These criteria are not applicable just to archeology, but to anthropology and to other social sciences as well. Specifically, archeology should espouse goals that limit the number of variables studied in a given piece of research; that require explication and explanation; that strengthen the ties between archeology and other social sciences, rather than weaken them; and that emphasize the unique aspects of archeological data rather than those aspects shared with all social data.

Archeology should select goals that limit the number of variables a given investigator must treat. Successful sciences are those in which there is agreement on a restricted number of variables to which all research is at least indirectly relevant. That is, most research either is carried out in terms of this set of variables or can be related to them. The variables a discipline treats change over time. But Kuhn's (1962) discussion of the importance of the paradigm makes it clear that in a discipline such as physics, the vast majority of scientists at a given time are working on a limited set of problems related to a few central models.

The construction and use of such models makes possible generalizations and explanations transcending the work of a single investigator. One difficulty in attempting to explain anything in anthropology is the fact that few tasks of data collection are comparable. Archeology tends to be defined by the department in which the scholar received his training.

An archeologist attempting to formulate and test a law to explain the occurrence of a particular set of phenomena often runs up against a brick wall in that he can find few other investigators who have collected data pertinent to the solution of his problem. By focusing on a few theoretical models and limiting to a finite set the number of critical variables in collecting data, archeologists can overcome this difficulty.

Approaches focusing upon explaining phenomena should be preferred over approaches that have the primary effect of data accumulation. Explanation in this sense means formulating and using laws to render predictable the occurrence of a particular phenomenon in a particular place at a particular time. A frequent tendency in archeology is to view explanation as a linear function of the amount of data collected and the time spent analyzing data. A particular piece of research that only accumulates data is justified on the grounds that it will someday lead to an explanation even if none is proposed within the context of the study.

This Baconian viewpoint has been dead in other disciplines for many years. Good explanations result from inspired guesswork, and from research that tests the validity of explanations. Data collection is a step in the process of explaining, and a research design that does no more than collect data is but a tiny bit of the research process. Unstructured data collection is more likely to involve a discipline in chaos than in explanation (see Kuhn 1962:16).

Goals that strengthen the relationship between archeology and other social sciences should be valued over goals that weaken this relationship. Archeologists often say we are social scientists and anthropologists. If this is the case, then our goals should reflect our identities. But more than intellectual honesty is involved—for when we formulate goals consistent with those of other social sciences, we can utilize the findings of these sciences in our own work.

Goals that emphasize the unique aspects of archeological data should be preferred over goals that do not. I am in complete agreement with Binford (1964:425) when he states that the range of cultural processes inferrable in the present are inferrable in the past. Nevertheless, within this range there are phenomena archeologists can study well and phenomena they can study only poorly.

For example, Chang (1967b) has argued that archeologists should study the relationship between artifacts and the mental templates or norms that must have existed in the minds of those who made the artifacts. Binford (1967:334) has labeled this process paleopsychology and noted that psychology is a subject for which archeologists are poorly equipped. Clearly, if an investigator is interested in the relationship between norms and the behavioral or material patterns through which these norms are expressed, this relationship can be studied far more easily in the present than in the past. In the present, norms and their material consequents can be studied independently, and hypotheses concerning their relationship formulated and tested. For the past, norms must be inferred from the same data that will be used to infer the material consequents of these norms. When such a technique is used, there are no independent data, and the relationship in question is not subject to testing, much less to explanation.

A second example is the goal of reconstructing past lifeways (Ascher 1961). Clarke (1968:13) comments on this goal as follows:

> The reconstruction of a historical or social picture of prehistoric cultures, written in historical narrative, is a valid but incidental and dangerous aspect of archaeology. Although aesthetically satisfying in the familiarity of its form of expression it is necessarily as ephemeral and as reliable as the facial expression reconstructed on the bones of a Neanderthal skull.

Again, if we are trying to portray total pictures of peoples at different levels of technological or cultural complexity, then we can meet this goal far more easily in the present than in the past.

Strengthening the relationship between archeology and anthropology and other social sciences is not the same as trying to do with prehistoric data the same sorts of things social scientists working in the present do with their data. Rather, we should be concerned with attempting to explain relationships difficult or impossible to study in the present, but for which prehistoric data provide a strong possibility of solution. Harris (1968:361) has argued that archeology ought to be more anthropological, but this does not mean it should strive to study the same phenomena that social anthropologists do, or to use the same techniques or even the same models.

> The really important questions which need answering are those which relate a population's pattern of material existence to its habitat over time periods sufficiently ample to shed light on the interaction between technology, economic behavior, and the "etic" organizations or groupings with which these are associated. The great strength of archeology is that it can deal with groups which are defined by the actual coming together and working together or living together of specific individuals at specific times and places. . . .

Other criteria could be mentioned in relation to evaluating goals, but these seem the most consistent with the kinds of statements archeologists are making about their discipline. They represent an attempt to objectify what is largely implicit when we argue for a greater role for explanation, or when we argue that archeology is a social science. In any case, they provide a basis for initiating a discussion of goals and a means for evaluating a particular goal that I now wish to discuss.

The Study of Change

Beyond this point, I am making no pretense of objectivity in discussing archeological goals. The discussion turns to what seems a most suitable goal for archeologists to pursue, not in the belief that it provides a final solution to the problem of archeological anomie, but that it is *a* solution, and that the time to begin discussing goals in the concrete has arrived.

Archeologists can fruitfully focus our research upon this question: Why do cultures change as they do? In other words, explaining change should be our primary undertaking.

Braidwood has effectively directed archeology toward the study of change. (See also Binford 1962; Childe 1951; Kluckholn 1967; Steward 1955; and White 1959.) While this orientation is clear throughout his work, it is perhaps most evident in the article, "Introduction to Archaeology," in the *Encyclopedia Britannica* (1968). Braidwood suggests that the primary task of archeology should be to understand the following: the emergence of anatomically modern man and the culture associated with his appearance, the origin of food production, the origin of civilization, and the comparison of these transformations and of modern transformations man is undergoing. Braidwood (1968:226) emphasizes the critical importance of the time factor:

> Given the enormous time depth with which only archaeology is prepared to deal, what can we learn of the changing relation between man, society and culture on the one hand and environment on the other; what of the generalized cultural processes which, because of the bearing of this time factor can be examined in no other way.

The works of Marshall McLuhan also suggest what a fruitful topic for analysis the examination of change can be. McLuhan is not a sophisticated social scientist; he is much more a hypothesis generator than a hypothesis tester. His work, nevertheless, does more than any other I know to demonstrate the complex interrelationship of environment, technology, culture, and behavior. He examines variables

from climate to thought processes, from tool-using to type of government, and is able to show close relationships between many of these.
His publications might have been written by an archeologist. They
have not been, and to that extent archeologists have failed to understand as well as someone from outside the discipline the relationship
between man's tools and man's behavior. McLuhan has shown the
value of multivariate analyses of culture change, and his work should
be regarded as a rich source of hypotheses for testing.

Furthermore, McLuhan's research emphasizes the timeliness of
studying change. Major technological transformations are occurring
more and more frequently and requiring less and less time to occur.
(See also Toffler 1970.) From the appearance of tool-using hominids
to the Neolithic transformation was a period of hundreds of
thousands of years. A few thousand years passed between the Neolithic and urban transformations. The industrial revolution in some
parts of the world followed the urban transformation by centuries
and for most of the world by a few thousand years. Now, McLuhan
argues, the electronic transformation is upon us. He and other
analysts have argued that similar transformations will occur with increasing rapidity.

Clarke's (1968) *Analytical Archaeology* demonstrates quite clearly the
close relationship between understanding change and doing archeology. Clarke defines archeology as the science of the artifact. But,
when he begins to create models for explaining artifactual variability, he finds it necessary to discuss models that concern change in
general, not just artifact change. The result is a thorough discussion
of systemic approaches to the study of change.

Braidwood argues that the study of change should be a primary
concern of archeologists. McLuhan shows us what a fruitful undertaking this sort of study can be. With Clarke we see the study of
change to be an almost inevitable outcome of doing archeology. I now
wish to suggest in more specific terms what I regard as the nature of
this undertaking.

As I have indicated, I believe that the basic question to which we
should address ourselves is: Why do cultures change as they do? Why
are some instances of change slow and others rapid? Why are some
accomplished with great ease and others with only the greatest difficulty? The answers to all such questions probably involve a limited
set of variables.

In emphasizing the importance of answering these questions in the long run, I want to stress the need for constructing models and providing explanations of change that transcend the isolated case. I am asserting that certain variables critical to individual instances of change are also important to change in general. Models that can explain change in both the near and the distant past will be of most value in analyzing change in the present and the future. The essential problem is to isolate variables of recurring importance in change, to explain the relationship between these variables, and thereby to use laws in explaining why cultures change as they do in specific instances.

This goal—the explanation of change—is consistent with the criteria earlier proposed as bases for evaluating the explanations that archeologists could undertake.

First, the pursuit of this goal would limit to a relevant few the number of variables critical to archeological research in general, that is, those critical to understanding change. Ideally, most archeological research would center around these variables, even if not in the specific context of studying change. With a focus on a few explanatory models, and therefore, a greater complementarity in research results, archeology's potential for explaining prehistory, as well as for being a contributing social science, would be greatly enhanced.

Second, pursuing this goal would necessitate going beyond description. The emphasis here would be placed on explaining change and on isolating variables critical in more than one instance of change. In no way can description in and of itself provide an answer to the questions posed as the crux of the goal. In short, the goal is to explain change, not to describe it.

The study of change is one of the few unifying topics in social sciences today, and such an undertaking would strengthen ties between archeology and other social sciences. Perhaps the greatest area of concrete interaction between social scientists of different disciplines is the study of the underdeveloped world. When one finds interdisciplinary courses being taught, they often concern modernization and development. When an interdisciplinary team goes into the field, the sponsoring agency is often linked with promoting development in some country. Whatever particular phenomenon a given discipline studies, it is always interested in changes in that phenomenon. And today, the study of change has taken the form of analyzing processes of modernization both in the underdeveloped world and in underdeveloped subgroups within our own culture.

Archeology offers the possibility of approaching the study of change in a different manner from other social sciences, the opportunity to test the relationship between variables in independent situations and in the long run. Virtually all the theories and laws of change proposed to date have been formulated and tested within the specific context of the transition from agriculture to industrialization, of a massive industrialized civilization confronting small, agricultural civilizations.

Because of the extreme relatedness of the situations in which these theories were developed or tested, the probability that they will be sufficient for studying the next instance of change is low. To repeat, all describe the particular case of the Western-directed industrialization of the underdeveloped world during the past few decades. It would be naive to assume that all change will include the same relationship between the same variables that obtains in this special case.

Archeologists must begin to discuss our goals and to better focus our aggregate activities. We should seek to explain phenomena other social sciences have difficulty explaining, but in which social science is interested. I and the archeologists I cited have argued that the study of long-term change is probably the most appropriate goal for archeologists to pursue.

It is difficult, even impossible, for social scientists working in the present to collect data that are both adequate and appropriate to the study of change. Not only must the investigator visit and revisit the field site—but the changes occurring there may be revealed only over a period of time greater than his lifetime. Moreover, it is not always possible to distinguish between a cyclical fluctuation and an irreversible change. If the archeological record is anything, it is a record of long-term change. And, to the extent that archeologists have failed to make use of this record, our failure can be traced to an overwillingness to borrow the largely synchronic models of change that the ethnologist employs.

CHAPTER TWO

Archeological Methods

The goals, techniques of inquiry, and data that characterize a discipline should be determined by conscious and explicit decisions. There must be harmony among the three. Moreover, decisions about goals, techniques of inquiry, and appropriate data are internal to a discipline.

Decisions about method are only partially internal to a discipline. Rules of evidence and standards of verification are good or bad not for a particular discipline, but for science as a whole. This point is made clear by Rudner (1966:5) in his *Philosophy of Social Science:*

> To become aware that various scientific disciplines employ differing techniques of investigation is not to become aware of anything significant about the nature of social science. . . . To claim that there is a difference in the *methodology* between two disciplines or two types of disciplines is, by contrast, to make a radical claim. For the methodology of a scientific discipline is not a matter of transient techniques but of its *logic of justification.* The method of a science *is,* indeed, the rationale on which it bases its acceptance or rejection of hypotheses or theories. Accordingly, to hold that the social sciences are methodologically distinct from the nonsocial sciences is to hold not merely (or perhaps not at all) the banal view that the social sciences

employ different techniques of inquiry, but rather the startling view that the social sciences require a different logic of inquiry. To hold such a view, moreover, is to deny that all of science is characterized by a common logic of justification in its acceptance or rejection of hypotheses or theories.

Archeologists have spent as much time trying to justify remaining outside an ongoing discussion of scientific method as in attempting to see whether or not our discipline could live by the same standards employed in others. How else can one explain the fact that doctrinaire Baconian inductivism finds its most vigorous, if not its only modern, proponents among archeologists? How else can one explain the major role that analogy, a form of argument universally labeled as the weakest, still plays in archeology? By discussing the nature of explanation and the acquisition and use of laws, I intend to show how archeology can carry on research within the established boundaries of good scientific method.

The Nature of Explanation

The subject of archeology is behavioral and cultural variability—the similarities and differences in behavior at specific temporal and spatial loci. Its object is to explain these similarities and differences. Explanation is a term that is used frequently by anthropologists in discussing research objectives. But, one rarely finds a consistent meaning in such usages. Moreover, this problem is not unique to anthropology.

Our disagreement over the meaning of explanation is a reflection of similar disagreement among epistemologists and philosophers of science. Viewed from different philosophical perspectives, explanation can have very different meanings. Yet, all definitions of explanation are attempts to provide models for knowing and knowing that one knows. Much of the variation in definitions of explanation reflects the varying emphases that different authors place on three components of the knowledge process: (1) the problem of constructing valid arguments; (2) the problem of constructing arguments that account for observed variability; and (3) the problem of insuring that the observed variability in both topic and causal variables is indeed observed and not a product of bias in techniques of data collection or analysis. (I have not included discovery in this list. While this topic is critically important, I know of no really successful attempts to explain or even define this phenomenon.) Within the context of these varying emphases, it is possible to define a number of diametrically opposed schools: deductivists versus inductivists; formalists versus substantivists; argumentivists versus correlationists; and so on. It will be argued that explanation that fails to place equal emphasis on all three components of explanation, explanation that fails to include deductive and inductive arguments, formal and correlational techniques, is incomplete.

The Formal Component: Constructing Valid Arguments

Philosophers concerned with the formal component of explanation are defining the classes of statements of which an argument is composed and analyzing the logical relationships that must exist between these classes of statements in order that an argument be deemed valid.

The model of explanation in this formal context which I have found most useful is the Hempel-Oppenheim, or deductive–nomological, model. In this model, an explanation is an argument that fits a phenomenon "into a pattern of uniformities and shows that its occurrence was to be expected given specified laws and pertinent particular circumstances [Hempel 1966:50]." Three classes of statements are used in constructing the argument: (1) statements about the phenomenon under investigation; (2) statements about pertinent particular circumstances; and (3) statements of laws. The last two types of statements are called the explanans, ". . . the class of those sentences that are adduced to account for the phenomenon [1966:51]." The explanandum is a sentence describing the phenomenon under investigation.

An explanation in this model looks like this:

$$L_1, L_2, \ldots \ldots L_n \quad \text{General Laws}$$
$$C_1, C_2, \ldots \ldots C_n \quad \text{Statements of Antecedent Conditions}$$

Logical
Deduction _____

Description of the
Empirical Phenomenon
to Be Explained

Having built such a skeleton, one turns to linkages, relationships that must exist between the propositions if they are to be considered valid. Philosophers have specified that the propositions must share certain terms. Moreover, the order of the terms in the proposition is critical—denying the first term (antecedent) or affirming the second (consequent) produces invalid arguments.

A primary question that arises from this model of explanation concerns the term, law. It seems pointless to engage in the old debate over the existence of anthropological (behavioral and cultural) laws—behavioral scientists use such laws explicitly and implicitly. A more important question concerns the sources of such laws, or at least statements that are worth testing because they might be laws. Miller's (1965b) "Living Systems: Cross-Level Hypotheses" and *Human Behavior: An Inventory of Scientific Findings* by Berelson and Steiner (1964) are excellent sources of such propositions. The ultimate source is of course the mind of the investigator attempting to create the knowledge. Hanson (1965) has written a provocative discussion of the discovery process.

The Substantive Component: Accounting for Observed Variation

Explanation in substantive terms means decomposing and accounting for variability in some phenomenon under investigation. Anthropologists deal with variations in behavior and cultural processes at different spatial loci at a single point in time, variations in culture and behavior at different points in time at a single spatial locus, and variations in culture and behavior at different points (usually parallel) at multiple spatial loci. In dealing with spatial phenomena, it is argued that the phenomenon under study has some patterned spatial distribution. In dealing with temporal phenomena, the variable forms a trace, or trajectory, over time. Explaining variability means developing the ability to predict or retrodict the spatial pattern or the shape of the trace, whichever is relevant.

The process of substantive explanation involves placing a phenomenon in a system of antecedent and intervening phenomena, placing a variable in a system of antecedent or intervening variables. These act and interact to cause the topic phenomenon to vary as it does. One might, for example, be interested in explaining changes in the population of a community over time. The topic variable might be the actual population at some series of points in time, or increments of populations per unit of time, or any of the various measures of rates of population change. Having chosen one or a number of measures as topic variables, a list of phenomena in the social and natural environments of the community that are viewed as potential determinants of population change is compiled and measurements instruments are developed for each of them. Holding all other variables constant, the relationship between each antecedent or intervening variable and the topic variable is considered. So are interaction effects. Statistics such as the partial correlation coefficient are used to tell the investigator in a reasonably precise fashion the percentage of the variability accounted for by a particular antecedent variable. The square of the multiple correlation coefficient indicates the percentage of variation in a topic variable that the entire system of variables under investigation accounts for. It is rarely possible to account for 100% of the variability in behavioral phenomena, but correlational techniques provide an investigator with a measure of his success in reaching this goal.

Simulation models provide an even more significant solution to the problem. The simplest of these is the linear regression model, in which the equation, $y = a + bx$, is used to define the relationship between a topic and antecedent variable. Multiple regression techniques allow for the analysis of a number of variables and permit the investigator to control for intervening variables and interaction effects. By specifying a series of variables and defining the relationship between them, in a statistical or formal simulation model, the investigator should be able to generate a trace for population change that very closely resembles the one that was observed.

The Operational Component: Finding Variation and Keeping It Observed

The operational component of explanation goes further in coming to grips with the whole activity or process of explaining, of doing research. Therefore, somewhat more attention will be devoted to it. Operational explanation is testing particular arguments or models. Operational definitions of explanation specify the classes of activities that constitute research and the way in which these activities should be ordered if an explanation is the desired product of the research. On the one hand, they specify a set of procedures to be used in identifying patterns of variation that may not be directly observable. On the other, they attempt to insure that the variability with which an investigator works is in fact observable and not a product of bias in the techniques of observation or analysis that he uses. The operational definition of explanation that I have found most useful specifies the following activities: formulation of a problem; formulation of hypotheses; operationalization of the hypotheses; collection of data; analysis; testing; and evaluation.

Such a research design must be followed in the order presented. Some people argue one can begin at any point in the list and still do valid research as long as each of the steps is ultimately carried out. This viewpoint is probably not useful because the single most important factor in formulating a research strategy and in acquiring and analyzing data is an hypothesis to which both are adapted; we do not collect or analyze data in a vacuum. We collect those data we see as relevant to the *solution of a particular problem* and analyze those aspects of data we see as relevant to the *solution of a particular problem.* Hempel (1966) makes this point very clear:

> What particular sorts of data it is reasonable to collect is not determined by the problem under study, but by a tentative answer to it that the investigator entertains in the form of a conjecture or hypothesis ... [p. 12].

> If a particular way of analyzing and classifying empirical findings is to lead to an explanation of the phenomena concerned, then it must be based on hypotheses about how those phenomena are connected; without such hypotheses, analysis and classification are blind [p. 13].

It is sometimes argued that one need not worry about the absence of explicit hypotheses because all research has implicit ones. Kluckholn (1939) asserted many years ago that no one collects data in the absence of some theoretical orientation that causes him to collect some data and ignore others. But, a fundamental identity usually exists between good research and research that has been done according to a well-planned design. When part of the research process is implicit, explicit consideration of the viability of the research design is unlikely.

Having made clear that the order of steps in the research is not arbitrary, I now want to discuss it in detail.

PROBLEM FORMULATION

At this first stage in the research process, the problem to be investigated is formulated in such a way that data and/or solutions to the problem are suggested. That is, statements like, "I am interested in culture change," or, "I am interested in Southwestern prehistory," are replaced by at least relatively precise questions: "Why did horticulturists living on the Colorado Plateau at about A.D. 700 begin to adopt water control techniques?" Formulating the problem should always involve an extensive review of the literature pertaining to the problem. It is often the case, and has too often been the case in the past, that the problem centered on a set of data: a site that an archeologist had been told to dig, a region he has been asked to survey. I assume that archeology is beyond the point where problems focused primarily on data collection are likely to be productive. None of anthropology's subdisciplines are lacking in either available data or research situations. To select a research site and to claim to be interested in "all of the variability that can be observed there" is naive and results in the rambling monographs that have been the bane of the discipline. Data sets and research settings must be selected with a problem in mind.

FORMULATION OF HYPOTHESES

Hypotheses are statements of relationship between two or more variables. They usually take the form, "if x, then y," and may be regarded as potential—but unproven—laws. At a minimum, they are potential solutions to the problem that has been formulated. The acquisition of hypotheses may occur within the context of an ongoing attempt to solve a particular problem or it may occur in the context of a fresh start on an essentially new problem. In the first case, the hypotheses with which one will be dealing are likely to be suggested conclusions of past research. In the second case, potential solutions to an essentially new problem may be original abductions or may be found in the literature of archeology, of anthropology, of the social sciences, or of general systems theory.

When the hypotheses upon which a given piece of research will be based are the suggested conclusions of past research, they are outgrowths of the sixth step in the research design: reformulation and evaluation of research. In this sense, the research design is part of an ongoing process. Nevertheless, it is still an integral unit within that research process, a unit that cannot be arbitrarily divided.

When hypotheses are acquired in a situation of approaching a new problem, they generally come from three sources: abduction, the literature of social sciences, or general systems theory.

Abduction is the perception that two or more variables may be related and that this relationship may explain the occurrence of the phenomenon under examination. It is the process of perceiving patterns in data (Hanson 1965:86–87; Hempel 1966:15). The quality of a given abduction is explained by the creative ability of an individual scientist.

Abduction is not induction. Good abductions do not depend upon the quantity of data a given investigator has examined. As Hempel (1966:15) points out,

> The transition from data to theory requires creative imagination. Scientific hypotheses are not *derived* from observed facts, but *invented* in order to account for them. They constitute guesses at the connections that might obtain between the phenomena under study, at uniformities and patterns that might underlie this occurrence.

Familiarity with data is an essential condition for carrying out any research, for operationalizing any hypothesis. But, while familiarity is essential, the probable validity of an hypothesis cannot be evaluated on the basis of the amount of data an investigator treated in creating it. It is a function of his creative ability as a scientist, and no more. One often suspects that those who wish to explain hypothesis creation as a linear function of data examination are trying either to shift responsibility for hypotheses they could not create or to protect themselves lest they be wrong. The courage to risk being wrong is the essence of innovation. And, to claim that explanations are derived from data rather than the minds of scientists is intellectual cowardice.

Hypotheses may be indicated conclusions of the research of other archeologists, anthropologists, or social scientists. That is, one may be using the abductions of others. In trying to solve a particular problem, one approach is seeing what conclusions one's co-researchers have reached about that problem or about related problems. An important resource in this activity is Berelson and Steiner's (1964) *Human Behavior: An Inventory of Scientific Findings.* This book presents 1000 hypotheses concerning problems with which social scientists frequently deal and summarizes the research that has been done in attempting to solve these problems. It treats no problem in sufficient detail to be a final authority, but it suggests some testable hypotheses representing potential solutions to specific problems and also provides references to research conducted on these problems.

OPERATIONALIZING THE HYPOTHESES

The kinds of operational procedures that an investigator will use will vary with the problem and field setting. There are, however, important steps that must be taken in operationalizing any set of arguments. (1) Test implications of the arguments must be identified. The investigator should specify particular states and conditions of, or patterns in, collectable data that he should find if the arguments he is proposing are valid. Any worthwhile argument should have observable implications, and it is to these implications that the investigator should direct his attention. (2) The data that must be collected in the field to determine whether the predicted states, conditions, and patterns are present should be specified. (3) Measurement devices for converting raw data to variables should be identified, and their efficacy demonstrated. Raw field data are bundles of attributes some of which are relevant to the investigator and some of which are not. Devices for observing and measuring the specific attributes of behavior that are relevant to the test implications must be specified. (4) A technique for insuring that there is no bias, or at least that there is a statable bias, in the data that investigator collects must be developed. The investigator must know the relationship between the sample of behavior that he observes and the behavioral universe. This concern need not imply random sampling. It is my impression that for most anthropological problems, random sampling is useful only within a factorial design, a design stratified by antecedent variables.

All social scientists, archeologists no exception, make conclusions about human behavior and cultural processes on the basis of samples. Few archeologists who do survey work can legitimately claim to have found all the sites in the surveyed area and few digs attempt the complete excavation of even a single site. Generalizations are made about the area surveyed on the basis of the sample and about the site on the basis of a partial excavation. Yet, these generalizations are often made without adequate concern with the nature of the sample taken. Archeologists have begun to give more attention to sampling (see Heizer and Graham, 1967; and Hill, 1965). An excellent discussion of various techniques of sampling appears in Haggett's (1966) *Locational Analysis in Human Geography*. I do not want to describe here the various kinds of mathematical sampling techniques, as these have been discussed in the volumes cited above. However, I do intend to summarize why such techniques of sampling should be used in testing. Recall that by this point in the research design hypotheses have already been generated.

When an investigator is not concerned with sampling, there is no guarantee his results are based upon reliable data. If he selects units he believes are typical, "typical" is subjectively defined when it should be defined on the basis of objective mathematics. If the universe is not defined, if the sample size is unknown, and if sites are not selected in a rigorous manner, the conclusions may warrant little confidence. If sites are selected because they are easily accessible or because they have some special characteristic, or if a survey is limited to a small portion of the area about which generalizations will be made, the presumption must be that the results are biased. If on the other hand, the survey is designed so as to assure that the total range of areas used by a culture will be investigated and the study area will be regularly sampled, the chances of bias are minimized. More important, when techniques of mathematical sampling are employed, the probability that the conclusions might be based on sampling error exists, but bias can be stated.

Second, sampling saves time. When the universe is defined, the proportion of it that must be sampled in order to collect enough cases to support statistically valid conclusions can be calculated. When the universe is not known, the investigator has no basis for limiting his data collection and may waste time collecting and processing unneeded data.

Finally, when an investigator is not concerned with sampling, he may limit the ability of his discipline to improve itself. One way in which any discipline improves its understanding of the phenomena it studies is by using new techniques and new theories on old problems. When unneeded data are collected, data are taken away from future investigators who might be interested in reworking a problem. By sampling, and thereby leaving some information in the ground, an investigator insures the availability of data in its original context for use by future colleagues.

ACQUISITION OF DATA

Acquisition is the mechanical process of deriving from the field the data that will be used to test an hypothesis. What data are to be collected and how they are to be collected have already been specified.

The specific techniques of data collection will vary with the problem under investigation.

There has been a point of view in archeology suggesting that absolute standards are appropriate to all situations of data collection. The inaccuracy of this view is indicated by the following comments on what have been archeological bibles: Wheeler's (1950) *Archaeology from the Earth* and Heizer's (1967) *A Guide to Archaeological Field Methods.* Chang (1967a: 129–130) comments on Wheeler:

> If a piece of archaelogical work is "aimed at recovering information bearing on man's cultural antecedents [Ackerman and Carpenter 1963:13]," it should then be evaluated on that basis rather than on the neat or sloppy appearance of a site during the excavations. I do not share in Mortimer Wheeler's advice that "on approaching an excavation, the trained observer can at a glance evaluate its efficiency. It is an axiom that an untidy excavation is a bad one [1955:80]." Neatness is preferable to untidiness, not a priori on aesthetic grounds but only if it enhances the effectiveness of the information-retrieval processes. Things have an order of significance, and a tidy excavation is not necessarily a good one.

In a recent review of Heizer and Graham's updated version of *A Guide to Archaeological Field Methods,* Binford (1968b:807) argued that,

> It approaches archaeological field work from the perspective of excavation procedure with little attention to the problem of scientific data collection as such. It is frequently asserted that certain types of observations are "important" yet there is little discussion of why they might be important or what relevance various types of information may have in the investigation of the past.

Excavating beautifully for the sake of beautiful excavations is no longer a justifiable goal. In the absence of a complete work that approaches the task of excavation from the point of view of valid techniques of data collecting, it is probably safest to take the position that we should employ techniques of data collection most appropriate to the particular sorts of data we are trying to collect. This does not mean data in which we are not interested should be ignored or discarded; we have an obligation to save the data we would destroy or whose context we would destroy. However, the Archives of Archaeology and similar repositories offer a mechanism for saving unused data without having to study it carefully and to analyze it in the same manner as relevant data.

ANALYSIS OF DATA

Analysis is the process whereby data from the field are put into the form in which they will be used in testing hypotheses. The analysis undertaken will relate to the definition of variables provided in the first step of the research design. Analysis may involve counting or factor analysis. One might need to do no more than count the number of sites with kivas. On the other hand, it might be necessary to make and record a score of measurements for each of several thousand stone tools. There is no set list of acts one performs in analysis—what occurs is determined by the problem under investigation.

TESTING OF HYPOTHESIS

Testing means studying the data to determine whether the predictions as to how data should look if the hypothesis were valid have been accurate or inaccurate. If the predictions are accurate, then the test of the hypothesis is considered positive. If the predictions are inaccurate, the hypothesis is considered to have been negatively tested. Testing will frequently, but not necessarily, involve the use of statistical techniques to measure the degree of association between variables.

Testing makes the difference between an hypothesis and a law. A law is a positively tested hypothesis. One negative test is enough to suggest that a particular hypothesis is probably not a law. One positive test, however, is not enough to make an hypothesis a law. A given piece of research is likely to involve one thorough test of a hypothesis. Therefore, more than one piece of research is necessary before a hypothesis can be considered a law.

This fact should not lead to the conclusion that the more times a particular hypothesis is tested, the greater the probability of its validity; the validity of an explanation is not a function of the quantity of data used in testing it. In the first place, such a view fails to take into account the law of large numbers—the increment to validity from each new piece of positive data is less than the preceding bit of data until the increment nears zero. Furthermore, this viewpoint fails to recognize the importance of variety and diversity.

More important than trying to add to the number of specific cases supporting a given hypothesis is deducing and testing predictions about *different kinds of data that bear on the hypothesis*. The independence of the tests for a given hypothesis is more important than their number. To test the proposition, if x, then y, enumerating 15 cases in which x and y are associated in the predicted manner would be a form of testing. A better form of testing would be deducing from the proposition, if x, then y, the test implications that if the proposition is valid then the following equalities should hold: $a = b$, $c = d$, $e = f$, $g = h$, and $i = j$, where $a \ldots j$ are independent classes of data shown to be related to the proposition, if x, then y, in multiple, independent cases. Testing on independent evidence does more to establish validity than testing that involves the repetitive use of a single set of evidence.

EVALUATION OF THE RESEARCH

This step in the research design involves a recapitulation of the completed research. It should include a discussion of the outcome of the tests and of the weaknesses of the tests.

The probability that the hypotheses are laws is discussed. In this sense the research as a case of law discovery is examined. The extent to which the hypotheses offered insight into the phenomenon is also examined, and in this sense the research as a case of using a statement of law is reconsidered. Suggestions for future research on this problem, as well as suggestions of new problems the research raises, should be considered.

Summary

The research design I have discussed consists of the following steps:

1. Formulation of the problem
2. Formulation of hypotheses
3. Operationalization of hypotheses
4. Acquisition of data
5. Analysis of data
6. Testing of hypotheses
7. Evaluation of research

The design involves the use of both deduction and induction. To test an hypothesis, test implications are deduced from it. Induction comes into play when the test implications are compared with specific sets of data to determine whether or not the deductions stand the test of data.

The research design sets out to establish and/or use laws by performing experiments with potential laws. The essence of the process is the experiment—making a prediction about how specific classes of data should look if an explanation is valid, and then collecting the data to see if the prediction was accurate. One often hears the argument that experiments in the social sciences do not have the conclusiveness of experiments in the natural sciences because social science experiments lack replicability. I think this view is wrong and will attempt to demonstrate its lack of validity by performing such an experiment.

I and a number of other investigators have argued that it is important to follow these steps in the order listed. Research is a process characterized by feedback—the reformulation of arguments and models while research is underway, the redefinition of variables, etc. Especially when an investigator works on a single problem for many years, this retooling will be continual. However, at any stage in the research process, it is desirable to stick with a basic set of procedures. A precise record of reformulations and modifications of a research design is one of the investigator's most valuable tools in seeking and finding new directions.

Research must be formally, substantively, and operationally complete if it is to result in explanations of observed variation. It is possible to formulate elegant arguments that are substantively meaningless. It is possible to operationalize trivial hypotheses. It is possible to account for 98% of the variation in some phenomenon without understanding its behavior a whit. It is impossible to explain rigorously and to acquire understanding without being concerned with all three components of explanation.

CHAPTER THREE

The Problem

Chapters 1 and 2 focused on the goals and methods of archeology. Beyond this point, I do not intend to be explicitly concerned with either of these topics. The research that I will describe is an attempt to pursue the goals and to apply the method. The remainder of the work is, then, a test of the worth of the goals and the workability of the method.

This chapter and Chapter 5 describe the purpose of the research. Research in general has two aims: (1) solving some problem relevant to an investigator's discipline and (2) testing laws explaining the class of phenomena of which the problem is an example. In this chapter, I will focus on the phenomenon with which this research is concerned. In Chapter 5, I will present a model containing the hypotheses that might explain this phenomenon. The purpose of the research is both to offer insight into the phenomenon and to test potential laws relevant to the class of phenomena of which it is an example.

The Basketmaker–Pueblo Concept

The Basketmaker–Pueblo concept has been used by Southwestern archeologists for over 75 years in describing an important change that occurred in different parts of this area between A.D. 500 and A.D. 1000. A great deal of the "meaning" of this concept has been shared by all of the archeologists who have employed it. But, particular characteristics of the concept have received differential emphasis from archeologists as our goals and interests have changed. By examining the history of this concept in Southwestern archeology, we may see something of the changes in the interests and orientations of the archeologists working there and better understand how the concept will be employed in this research.

The Initial Formulation

Archeological research in the American Southwest during the 1870s, 1880s, and 1890s was carried out by a very mixed group of individuals, including government officials, local citizens, explorers, and representatives of several museums. The majority of these investigators were, at best, self-trained archeologists. Their attention focused on the cliff-dwellings and other large masonry structures that dotted the area. It was common to refer to the populations presumed to have constructed these buildings as the Cliff-Dwellers.

In 1891, a group of rancher–archeologists, including John Wetherill, Charles McLoyd, and Howard Graham (and, possibly, Richard Wetherill), exploring the Grand Gulch area of Utah encountered a series of caves that contained archeological materials very different from those associated with the Cliff-Dwellers. The evidence consisted substantially of burials that lacked the characteristic cranial deformation of the Cliff-Dwellers. Baskets rather than pottery were found with the burials (Gillmor and Wetherill 1953).

The Wetherills sensed that this evidence might be of a people earlier than the Cliff-Dwellers. During 1892 and 1893 further exploration by the Wetherills and their friends at caves in the Grand Gulch area and at Step-House in Mesa Verde produced stratigraphic evidence indicating that the Basketmakers, as they were called, were indeed representatives of a population that inhabited the area prior to the Cliff-Dwellers. This discovery produced only a limited archeological response. The Wetherill's work was discussed by Pruden (1897) and Pepper (1902). But, as late as 1912, when Kidder and Guernsey began their work in the Kayenta area of Arizona, the Basketmaker concept had had an insignificant impact on archeologists' thinking about Southwestern prehistory (Lister and Lister 1968).

The Developing Complexity[1]

Kidder and Guernsey's work was to establish the efficacy of the Basketmaker. In 1914 and 1915 they excavated in a series of caves that contained evidence of the Basketmaker. They defined this population on the basis of the absence of cranial deformation, the absence of pottery, and the presence of artifacts such as square-toed sandals, baskets, cradles, bags, and hair cordage. Moreover, Guernsey was able to definitively establish that the Basketmakers were earlier than the Pueblo (Lister and Lister 1968: 19–21).

At this point, the Basketmaker–Pueblo concept was used in reference to different "peoples" or "cultures." But, what was the relationship between these peoples? The Basketmaker had clearly inhabited the area prior to the Pueblo: Had they left prior to the arrival of the Pueblo, had they been displaced by the Pueblo, or were they the ancestors of the Pueblo?

Evidence bearing on these questions began to appear. In 1910, Cummings, working in the Kayenta area; in 1913, Morris, working in southwestern Colorado; and in 1914, Kidder and Guernsey, working in the Kayenta area, found evidence of a population with the characteristic Pueblo cranial deformation, but who lived in houses with slab foundations and jacal walls—the Slab-House Dwellers, or Pre-Pueblo. (Lister and Lister 1968: 57–64). In 1920, Guernsey discovered Basketmaker burials in clear association with Pre-Pueblo-like artifacts. Morris soon reported similar discoveries from Colorado (Lister and Lister 1968: 64–74). These were the Post-Basketmakers.

But, what of the relationship between the Pre-Pueblo and the Post-Basketmakers? Earl Morris's 1922 excavations at Site 19 in southwestern Colorado revealed evidence of Basketmaker skeletal material in clear association with Pre-Pueblo artifacts. The cultural transition from Basketmaker to Pueblo was now established (Lister and Lister 1968: 76–77). The concept could now be used in reference to a sequence of changes, rather than simply to the respective "peoples."

---

[1]The period about to be described was one of the most exciting in the development of Southwestern archeology, and these few paragraphs will hardly do it justice. In their biography of Earl Morris, Lister and Lister (1968) portray the events of this epoch in a fashion that will interest anyone concerned with the history of archeology. The summary presented here is taken from their lengthy discussion.

Systematization

The Basketmaker–Pueblo concept was systematized at the first Pecos Conference as reported by Kidder in 1927. Kidder broke the developmental sequence of Anasazi culture into the following stages: Basketmaker, Post-Basketmaker, Pre-Pueblo, Prehistoric Pueblo, and Modern Pueblo. Each stage was defined by associated traits more complex than those of the preceding stage. *The classification was intended as developmental, not as a spatial–temporal classification.* Space and time were components of the scheme, but its essential purpose was to isolate different levels of development.

Kidder believed the basic changes in the Anasazi region from the first centuries A.D. to the present were in house form, pottery, storage features, projectiles, agriculture, and head form. Over the stages, there were shifts from no permanent houses to above-ground masonry structures; from the absence of pottery to the presence of plainware, corrugated ware, black-on-white ware, and polychrome; from storage pits dug in cave floors to storage rooms in pueblos; from atlatl use to use of the bow and arrow; from minimal reliance on agriculture to heavy reliance on agriculture; and from dolicocephalic populations to brachiocephaly.

Kidder argued that the change in head shape represented the immigration of a new "people" into the Anasazi area. He viewed some domestication and technological innovations as contributions of these immigrants. Nevertheless, he argued that the basic developmental pattern was an indigenous one, that the brachiocephalic peoples added a number of essentially minor traits to a substantial base and contributed little to the changes in the developmental sequence Kidder first suggested.

Kidder's classification was modified by the first Pecos Conference and by Roberts (1935). Rouse (1966: 36–42) has presented an up-to-date revision of Roberts's scheme as follows:

Basketmaker: Agriculture (but not intensive) based on
                primitive forms of corn and squash. No
                pottery. Slab-lined storage cists. Houses
                in caves or made of wood set into saucer-
                shaped depressions. Cists used for storage
                and burial. Baskets. Bags. Sandals.
                Nets. Cords. Atlatl.

Modified Basketmaker:	Greater dependence on agriculture with beans and new varieties of corn. Pit dwellings lined with stone slabs. Pottery. Bow and arrow. More sedentism.
Developmental Pueblo:	Addition of cotton to the agricultural complex. Great architectural experimentation —slab houses, adobe houses, wattle and daub structures and multi-room masonry pueblos. Kivas. Black on white and corrugated pottery. Decline of basket making. Burial in refuse outside houses. Expansion of areal extent of the culture.
Great Pueblo:	Agriculture. Large multi-story masonry buildings. Black-on-white, corrugated and polychrome pottery. Highly developed ornamentation. Great regional specialization. High population mobility.
Regressive Pueblo:	Agriculture. Large Pueblos with central courts. Rectangular kivas. Elaborate painted or glazed wares. Concentration of population in a few centers.

Space–Time Systematics

Up to this point, the collection of specimens for museums had been the primary justification for field work. Increasingly, however, space–time typologies became a major focus, rather than a spin off, of the museum work. In the 1930s and 1940s, the attention of Southwestern archeologists turned: (1) to the derivation of more precise dates for the stages of the Basketmaker–Pueblo typology; (2) to specification of traits associated with each of the stages; and (3) to the exploration of the relationship between Basketmaker and Pueblo and prehistoric populations in other areas of North America. Little new knowledge was added to our understanding of the processes of change represented in the developmental typology. Instead, the typology was converted into a chronology.

Dating techniques developed since Kidder's formulation of the Basketmaker–Pueblo scheme have permitted archeologists to place the sequence in a chronological framework as follows:

Basketmaker	A.D. 1–400
Modified Basketmaker	A.D. 400–700
Developmental Pueblo	A.D. 700–1100

Great Pueblo	A.D. 1100–1300
Regressive Pueblo	A.D. 1300–1500
Historic Pueblo	A.D. 1500+

While these chronologic associations have some basic integrity, regional and local exceptions are important, and the temporal boundaries are nowhere as precise as the dates suggest. After all, the scheme is developmental, and Kidder never argued for an even pace of development in all areas of the Southwest. Neither did he envision the trait changes that he emphasized as covarying on a one-to-one basis. For most of the Anasazi region, there would be considerable error in inferring that because a site was occupied A.D. 700–1100, it must be Developmental Pueblo and must contain the precise list of associated traits.

The second topic of concern, traits, has not clarified but confused the developmental sequence. Many Southwestern archeologists have attempted to define in greater and greater detail each of Kidder's stages, associating more and more traits with the sequence. Such attempts are really aimed at replicating reality in greater and greater detail, not at explaining it. A glance at one such work (Reed 1964) shows that the more trivial the trait analyzed, the less it corresponds to any developmental scheme. Is there any good reason why wooden boxes, for example, should have a developmental sequence that closely parallels the sequence for agriculture or architecture?

The result of such trait analyses has been a series of impressionistically constructed lists implying spatial and temporal integrity, but rarely achieving either. If it is possible to clarify the extensive information concerning the spatial–temporal distributions of minute traits, it will be done by using appropriate statistical techniques to test the efficacy of the hypothesized covariation, not by impressionistically surveying available knowledge.

The most basic objection, however, to trait-list analyses is that even when they are successful, they do not explain. One explains by determining which traits are critical and which are not, not by treating all traits more or less equally.

A similar set of objections must be directed toward measures of the qualitative aspects of trait changes. McGregor (1965:472) graphed changes in the "general excellence" of traits in the Anasazi region from A.D. 1 to the present. He was presumably measuring the artistic ability or creative capacity of the inhabitants of the region and his graph of changes showed a dramatic increase in excellence at the time of the Basketmaker–Pueblo transition. However, since the dimensions that McGregor was measuring were unclear, his analysis added little to the understanding of general cultural development, much less to explaining the processes involved.

A final set of works concerns the role of diffusion in Southwestern prehistory. Additions to Southwestern trait lists have been traced to the East (Carter 1945:120), to the Mississippi Valley (Rouse 1966:37), and to Mexico (Jennings *et al.* 1956:74–75; Schroeder 1965).

Other than Kidder's developmental sequence, most explanations that have been offered for the transition proceed in terms of critical traits that were diffused from various parts of the New World. To date, no archeologist has succeeded in contradicting Kidder's basic argument that the change was essentially indigenous. Even had conclusive evidence concerning the diffusion of essential changes been discovered, one would still doubt that a true explanation had been provided, at least in the sense that the term, explanation, is being used in this volume.

"Diffusion" is a term that describes a historical event. Neither the term itself nor a set of data associated with it can answer the question of why some event occurred. To say that an event occurred because of diffusion is not to render the event predictable. A statement of the type, "all events of type x are caused by diffusion," is nonsensical.

This is not to say that the study of diffusion is not worthwhile. It is. However, from the theoretical perspective that underlies this volume, diffusion and independent invention are viewed as alternative historical mechanisms for effecting a particular law at a particular time and place. Steward (1955:182) has noted, "One may fairly ask whether each time a society accepts diffused culture it is not an independent recurrence of cause and effect." The task of this analysis will be to look for precisely these recurrent patterns of cause and effect.

From an Evolutionary Perspective

In the 1950s and 1960s, attention once again focused on the evolutionary implications of the Basketmaker–Pueblo typology. The typology has been seen as a reflection of change in the "level of organization" of local societies, and the basic importance of the shift from hunting and gathering to agriculture has been reemphasized.

Willey and Phillips (1958: 152–153) have viewed the changes in Kidder's sequence as a transition from an Archaic to a Formative level of organization. They see Basketmaker as a terminal Archaic adaptation and Modified Basketmaker and subsequent stages as Formative ones. While the cultural reality of concepts such as "Archaic" and "Formative" remains obscure, the value of this approach is in the reemphasis of the developmental nature of the original Basketmaker–Pueblo formulation.

Chang (1958) used the Southwest in his study of Neolithic social groupings. He emphasized the importance of the economic changes that were occurring at this time and suggested that a change from homesteads to unplanned villages to planned villages occurred. He associated these changes with a development from nonlineage to multilineage (intracommunity nonlocalized) to multilineage (intracommunity localized) to monolineage society.

Schoenwetter and Dittert (1968) approached developing Southwestern culture from an ecological viewpoint. They considered critical changes in land use, water use, population distribution, and water control systems that occur with the transition to Pueblo culture. While their analysis added valuable insight into the nature of the change by pointing to a new set of critical variables, the impact of the analysis was sharply reduced when they assigned environmental change the critical role of independent variable. One must question the worth of an explanation that dismisses many critical changes in Southwestern culture as accident. Schoenwetter and Dittert (1968) argued that "once the cultural change from a transient to a sedentary settlement form has been accomplished, the Anasazi found themselves the perpetrators more by accident than design of an ever elaborated system [p. 59]."

Tracing the fundamental changes in Southwestern culture to environmental change is not "wrong." Theories are rarely ever just plain wrong. Nevertheless, an explanation which can explain the changes in the variables that Schoenwetter and Dittert were concerned with, but which does not of necessity consign a whole set of other major changes to "accident," must be sought and preferred.

At present, we know the following about changes in Southwestern prehistoric culture. A major transformation occurred A.D. 500–1100. At a general level, this tranformation may be viewed as the shift from an essentially Archaic to an essentially Formative culture. More specifically, the adaptation to the mountainous Southwest and the Colorado Plateau was becoming more agricultural and sedentary. Major technological improvements occurred in pottery, hunting devices, architecture, and water control systems. There were major changes in settlement pattern. (While my research did not focus on the Basketmaker–Pueblo "heartland," but on an area that is transitional Anasazi–Mogollon, the sequence of change covered by the Basketmaker–Pueblo transition is reflected locally.)

Explaining the Transition

To explain the Basketmaker–Pueblo transition in a manner consistent with the definition of explanation discussed earlier, it is necessary to find the laws that render this kind of event—a transition—predictable. Explanation in terms of diffusion or independent invention is not explanation at all because the investigator is explaining the event by citing other events that occurred with, or prior to, it. As Spaulding (1968) has argued, ". . . the mere recitation of a list of successive events is not an explanation at all unless there are implicit laws or empirical generalizations linking the events [p. 35]." Knowing whether a set of laws is affected in a particular instance by diffusion or independent invention is less important than knowing what the laws are.

A search for the laws explaining the Basketmaker–Pueblo transition begins with a consideration of the kind of event the transition represents. I noted earlier that this event encompasses a major change in the economic base, from hunting and gathering to agriculture. In this sense, it is a part of a worldwide set of events—the Neolithic, or the transition from Archaic to Formative organization.

But, one can go further, for the Neolithic is itself one of a set of events. It is one of the great transformations or revolutions that has occurred during the human past. Thus, the search for laws to render predictable a specific set of events, the appearance of Pueblo culture, can best be sought at the level of the set of events of which the Southwestern transition is one example, at the level of understanding the nature of change during transformations.

CHAPTER FOUR

The Natural Laboratory:
Subsistence and Settlement
in the Upper Little Colorado

The transition is examined in a part of the Southwest that is generally referred to as the Upper Little Colorado. This region is bounded by the White Mountains on the south, Highway 63 between Show Low and Holbrook on the west, and the Little Colorado to the east and north. For the past 18 years, Paul S. Martin has directed the Southwest Archaeological Expedition of the Field Museum of Natural History in its research in the area. For the past 12 years, the Expedition has worked in Hay Hollow Valley on the Navajo county line, 12 miles east of Snowflake, Arizona.

The region is covered by three important plant–animal communities. Yellow pine parkland occupies most of the higher elevations. Elevations of 6000–7000 feet are usually covered by a juniper-pinyon woodland. Grassland communities are characteristic of lower elevations. Of course, over much of the region there is a complex interdigitation of these communities. The vegetation of the area has been described in greater detail by Hevly (1964).

The major drainage in the region is the Little Colorado, flowing northward from Springerville, and then turning westward above St. Johns. Most of the secondary drainages flow to the north, meeting the

Little Colorado after it has begun its westward course. The Little Colorado, before the construction of Lyman dam, was permanent nearly to St. Johns. Other drainages are impermanent, save in a few spring-fed localities along their reaches. Drainage has been disrupted and the land surface modified by vulcanism that occurred between 10,000 and 1 million years ago. Some parts of the central portion of the region are internally drained as a result of this vulcanism. Cooley (1964) has described the geography of the region in much greater detail.

The first human beings entered the Upper Little Colorado about 10,000 years ago. Prehistoric occupation lasted until about A.D. 1500.

The focus of the past decade of the Museum's research and of this work is one locality in the region, Hay Hollow Valley. Work has been done in an area of about 25 square miles lying just to the west of a basalt mesa known as Point of the Mountain. This mesa forms the eastern margin of the valley, while the western edge is marked by a series of sandstone mesas, somewhat lower than Point of the Mountain. The valley is drained by Hay Hollow Wash and its tributaries. Hay Hollow Wash is impermanent throughout its course. The locality is transitional between jupiter-pinyon woodland and grassland communities. The first human populations apparently entered the valley at about B.C. 1000. No sites that clearly date to an earlier period have been located. The valley was probably abandoned about A.D. 1300–1400.

Chronology of Hay Hollow Valley

Longacre (1964) has developed a chronology for the Upper Little Colorado, which I will not reproduce here. I do want to discuss the chronology of the Hay Hollow Valley, but this chronology is very different in certain respects from Longacre's. While the records for ceramics and chipped and ground stone tools are very similar there are some rather substantial differences in changes in settlement patterns. While I suspect these differences are largely the product of the much more intensive research done in the valley, it is impossible to account for them at present. The major phases in the occupation of Hay Hollow Valley are as follows.

PHASE I: 1500 B.C.–A.D. 300

Two sites of this phase were excavated in Hay Hollow Valley, the County Road site and the Hay Hollow site. Martin (1967:8) described the Hay Hollow site as follows:

> . . . most of the features fall into three major clusters, each separated from the others by one hundred feet or so. Each cluster contains from one to three houses, one to three large pits (6 to 12 feet in diameter) and many smaller pits, some of which served as hearths and some as storage . . . . Each house was round, about 16 feet in diameter, and was provided with a saucer-like dirt floor, the center slightly lower than the rim.

The Hay Hollow site was occupied 200 B.C.–A.D. 200. The County Road site was occupied at about 1000 B.C.; four houses have been excavated there. The configuration of both sites was very similar.

We have no reliable basis for estimating how many other sites of Phase I exist in the valley. While many "prepottery" sites were located in surveys in the valley, I am unwilling to make an immediate inference that all sites lacking pottery were indeed "prepottery." Some of them may have been, and probably were, limited-activity or special-use sites, where pottery simply was not used.

A few very crudely made brownware sherds were found at the Hay Hollow site. Projectile points from sites of this phase were predominantly stemmed-indented-base ones made on very thick flakes. Basin metates and cobble manos predominated.

While corn was recovered from these sites, subsistence was apparently based largely on hunting and gathering. Zubrow (1971a,b) has inferred that the social organization of this phase was of localized, unilateral, exogamous groups. Each house was probably the abode of a nuclear family.

PHASE II: A.D. 300–500

No sites of this phase have been excavated, although testing has been done at the Connie site and the Kuhn site. These sites were apparently occupied A.D. 200–700. Pithouses on the sites were somewhat smaller and deeper than those of the preceding phase. In some cases, they were encircled with a row of boulders. Both sites occurred on mesa tops. This contrasted significantly with the preceding phase, when sites were located on the valley floor, adjacent to Hay Hollow Wash.

Four habitation sites of Phase II have been located in Hay Hollow Valley, all on mesa tops. There were probably about eight such sites in the valley. (This figure is an extrapolation based on the percentage of the total area of the locality that has been sample-surveyed.) Although generalizing on the basis of four sites is risky, there seem to have been two different settlement sizes, one of fewer than 20 rooms, the other, of more than 50 rooms. Whether some centralization in the settlement pattern is indicated, or whether the smaller communities were occupied for a shorter period or occupied later in the phase, is a moot question.

Pottery was still not abundant in Phase II, but some Lino Gray and varieties of Alma were found. Stemmed and notched projectile points were found on the sites. A mixture of basin and trough metates and cobble and rectangular manos were found.

No data were available that would permit meaningful inferences concerning social organization. Subsistence was still based primarily on hunting and gathering, although agriculture may have been somewhat more important.

PHASE III: A.D. 500–750

The only excavated site of this phase in Hay Hollow Valley is the Gurley site, to be reported in this volume. The Gurley site, or perhaps better, Gurley sites, lay along the floor of the valley. They consisted of a series of loci, some of which were units of one or two pithouses, and others of which were limited-activity sites. None of these loci was over 20 m in diameter.

There were on the order of 40 such sites in the valley. The sites clearly fell into two categories: one type of settlement consisted of 1 or 2 pithouses, the second had over 10. Sites of the larger type occurred on the valley floor and were usually about 4 miles from each other, with settlements of the smaller type scattered in between. There was clearly a tendency to centralization in the settlement pattern of Phase III.

Lino Gray and varieties of Foresdale and Alma were the predominant ceramics. White Mound, Red Mesa, and Kiututhlanna Black-on-White were also found. Trough metates and small projectile points, side-notched and made on thin flakes, are characteristic of Phase III.

Evidence concerning social organization is still insubstantial. One of the houses at the Gurley sites was kivalike in its features. The larger pithouse villages may have been some kind of organizational center, but we may have also been observing a seasonal change in settlement pattern.

PHASE IV: A.D. 750–900

The only site of Phase IV that was excavated proved to be a limited-activity site. Large limited-activity sites seem to have been important during this phase. There were probably about 40 settlements in Hay Hollow Valley during Phase IV although only one size settlement was represented, that with a mean of four rooms. Some of the sites were pithouse communities, similar to those of the preceding phase; others were small pueblos. A great deal of architectural innovation and experimentation characterize Phase IV.

Pottery types of Phase III were abundant, but so was Snowflake Black-on-White. Occasionally black-on-red sherds were found on the sites. Projectile points, manos, and metates were similar to those of the preceding phase.

Apparently, there were no important central settlements during this period. Each site was the residence of more than one nuclear family, although it is not possible to specify the relationship between the families. Since organization was apparently changing in the direction of a matrilocal residence rule, the sites may represent small matrilocal units.

PHASE V: A.D. 900–1100

A number of sites of this phase have been excavated. The most important was Carter Ranch Pueblo, which has been described in detail by Martin, *et al.* (1964). Other sites included Site 137, a small, rectangular unit of 11 rooms; Site 430, a small, rectangular unit of 7 rooms; Site 511, an L-shaped unit of 14 rooms; and Site 83, a large, L-shaped unit, with outliers, of 40 rooms.

There were probably about 150 habitation sites in the valley during Phase V. These fell into three classes: the first had a mean of 1 habitation room; the second, a mean of 4 habitation rooms; and the third, a mean of about 17 habitation rooms. (These are means for habitation rooms, not total rooms on the site.) The one-room sites were located in situations that would be ideal for agriculture and probably represent some sort of "field house." The smaller sites might have been the abode of a single lineage or matrilocal group, while the larger sites were apparently the abode of many such groups. There was a clear hierarchy in the settlement pattern, and there was some tendency toward a centralized pattern—large sites were surrounded by smaller ones, which were in turn surrounded by field houses (Johnson 1970).

Artifacts were much the same as in Phase IV. Slab metates, however first appeared during this phase. Much more pottery of the Wingate Black-on-Red Show Low Black-on-Red types was found.

Subsistence was more heavily based on agriculture during Phase V than during any other phase, although hunting and gathering were still practiced. Saraydar has shown that the population of the valley was greater than would be expected on the basis of either hunting and gathering or rainfall farming (1970). Indeed, irrigation ditches that date to Phase V have been recorded, and there was some evidence that naturally and artificially terraced plots on the side of Point of the Mountain were used. In respect to social organization, there was evidence of settlements of several matrilocal groups. Kivas associated with these groups, as well as great kivas that might have been used by a whole village or several villages, were found.

PHASE VI: A.D. 1100–1400

The major excavated site of Phase VI was Broken K Pueblo, described by Martin *et al.* (1965). Broken K is a large pueblo of about 100 rooms. Other excavated sites included Site 201, an 80-room pueblo built around a plaza; Site 196, a 22-room, rectangular pueblo; and Site 195, an 11-room, rectangular unit. Site 201 was the only one of these sites with a great kiva.

There were probably about 35 habitation sites in the valley during this phase, with three classes of sites: one room "field houses"; multigroup pueblos of about 17 habitation rooms; and sites of 4-room blocks around a plaza, with an average of 57 habitation rooms. Most of the larger sites were built as the population in Hay Hollow began to decline.

During Phase VI, corrugated types were more important than plainwares. Black-on-white types were the most abundant of painted types, but black-on-red and polychrome types were also important. Slab metates and much larger, rectangular manos replace the grinding stones of the previous phase.

Hill (1965) has argued that this phase was characterized by a significant return to hunting and gathering, although agriculture remained the main means of subsistence. Hill has also discussed the evidence for matrilocal residence during the phase and other aspects of the extant social organization.

The discussion of these phases has been very much oriented to description, and the phase definitions have been very brief. The intent is to reflect my own disenchantment with a descriptive approach to the archeological record and, while I have provided the chronology as a customary introduction to the valley, the remainder of this volume will attempt to define a more meaningful approach to its prehistory.

Prehistoric Environmental Changes

It is clear that the environment of Hay Hollow Valley was very different from that of the present at certain points in the prehistoric past. Bohrer (1968) has discussed data suggesting that immediately before A.D. 200, and at A.D. 500–600, the valley was significantly wetter than at present. This conclusion is suggested by palynological and macrofaunal data from both the Hay Hollow and Gurley sites. *Typha* and *Equisetum* apparently grew in the valley when these sites were occupied. Hevly (1964) has studied the palynological record from the Upper Little Colorado and the valley in great detail. His conclusions are summarized in Table 4.1. Two basic patterns of variation were evident: an alternation between increased and decreased effective moisture; and between biseasonal and heavy summer rain-

TABLE 4.1
Climatic Conditions in the Upper Little Colorado[a]

Time period (A.D.)	Rainfall Intensity	Rainfall Distribution
200–400	Decreased effective moisture	Biseasonal rainfall
400–600	Increased effective moisture	Biseasonal rainfall
600–900	Decreased effective moisture	Biseasonal rainfall
900–1100	Increased effective moisture	Biseasonal at first, shifting to a heavy summer concentration
1100–1300	Decreased effective moisture	Summer rainfall pattern
1300–1500	Increased effective moisture	Biseasonal rainfall

[a]After Hevly 1964.

fall distribution. Reasonably high effective moisture and biseasonal distribution are most favorable to the growth of both wild and domesticated plants. In these terms, the periods A.D. 400–600 and A.D. 1300–1500 would have been most favorable; the periods A.D. 200–400 and A.D. 600–900, unfavorable. Between A.D. 1100 and 1300, when effective moisture was low and poorly distributed throughout the year, conditions were at their worst.

Subsistence

Throughout the now-known archeological record in Hay Hollow, hunting, gathering, and agriculture all yielded important dietary resources. Macrofloral, palynological, and faunal data were used in these reconstructions. Pollen data were taken from living floors, pits, hearths, jar and bowl fills, mano and metate washings, and, in one case, from the bed of an irrigation ditch. Unfortunately, there are no rockshelters in the valley, and it therefore has been impossible to obtain as detailed a record of subsistence change as is desirable. A few general statements can be made, however.

First, a variety of small animals were hunted throughout the valley's prehistory. The most important of these were deer and rabbit.

Second, agriculture has been practiced in Hay Hollow Valley from the time of the first sites, which are dated to 1000 B.C. While a quantified trend cannot be described, it is clear that the importance of domesticates increased over time. In the earliest sites, only corn was represented. By about A.D. 500, corn and squash were also grown. Irrigation ditches were used to water fields that certainly contained corn and cucurbits by A.D. 1000.

The record of gathered resources is known in some detail. At about A.D. 100, plants that were certainly exploited included *Chenopodium, Amaranthus, Opuntia, Ephedra, Pinus edulis, Graminae, Pertulacae,* and *Typha.* By A.D. 700, varieties of *Cycloloma, Cruciferae, Leguminosae, Typha, Equisetum,* and *Compositae* were also utilized. In addition, *Juglans* and *Oryzopis* were found at Carter Ranch site; and *Artemisia, Ephedra, Eriogonum, Rhus,* and *Sphaeralcea* were used at Broken K site. It is impossible to be certain that these changes are not the result of differential preservation, increasing sedentism, or the use of more rigorous techniques for the recovery of plant materials at sites excavated in the past few years. Most of these resources would be found in an early, dry cave site in surrounding areas.

CHAPTER FIVE

Models of Change

Attempting to explain the Basketmaker–Pueblo transition requires the development of one or more models of change—verbal constructs that isolate critical elements of the change and describe their interrelationships. In archeology, the chronology has been the most common model used in describing such changes. The weakness of this model has been noted by Adams (1966) and will be discussed below. Models of change used by anthropologists working with modern data are usually models of spatial, rather than temporal, variability, since most ethnographers employ almost exclusively synchronic data in their work. I have criticized ethnographic approaches to the study of change elsewhere (Plog 1972, in press a, in press b), and also noted the problems that have been generated when archeologists have attempted to use them. Suffice it to say that the temporal component of most ethnographic models is inferred, rather than observed, and the major components of such models specify devices for inferring change, rather than techniques for using data that describe sequence of change.

Archeologists do, of course, work with legitimately diachronic data. We have generally failed, however, to appreciate the uniqueness of these data for the social scientist. Nor have we been heavily committed to the process of picking up where other social scientists must leave off because they lack such data. Nor have we generally recognized the important role that the transition from synchronic to diachronic studies has played in the evolution of many of the natural sciences (Lewin 1935). In short, we have had a set of data that many other social scientists desire but cannot obtain, and we have failed to use the very qualities of the data that make them so desirable.

I will discuss throughout the remainder of this volume some of the subtle ways in which archeologists have been stopped short of a full use of the diachronic potential of their data. Here I wish to focus on the most basic of these problems, the chronology.

When an archeologist is asked to describe the pattern of change over time for the site or region he is studying, his basic response will be to create a chronology—to define a series of phases, stages, or periods, in short time blocks. To conceptualize time in this fashion is to treat it categorically. But, time is not a series of categories: It is a continuum. And the most appropriate representation of behavioral and cultural change in time that we can derive must take account of this fact. Clarke (1968) has discussed this point extensively and used terms such as "time trace" and "trajectory" in describing the continuous pattern of change over time in some variable. It should be evident that anthropology has no methodology for analyzing variables conceptualized in such a fashion. Unfortunately, other social sciences do not prove to be the source of such models. But before trying to develop some, let us first understand why and how chronologies lead archeologists astray.

A categorical typology is most useful when a set of observations can be placed in a set of categories in such a way that variability in the observations *within* categories is slight, while variability *between* categories is substantial. Thus, on a three-component site, an archeologist might describe one stratum that contains only artifacts a–e; a second, containing only f–k; and a third, containing only l–s. In fact, archeological data rarely meet such high standards of consistency. Artifacts are gradually replaced by other artifacts that serve the same or different purposes. The pattern we usually observe is similar to that in Figure 5.1. In this case, one might define Phase I by the presence of a, b, and c, Phase II by the presence of d, e, and f, and Phase III by g, h, and i. While no pattern of variation for a single artifact fits the overall pattern precisely, and some artifacts confound it entirely, there is less variability within, than between, categories.

Phase I   Phase II   Phase III

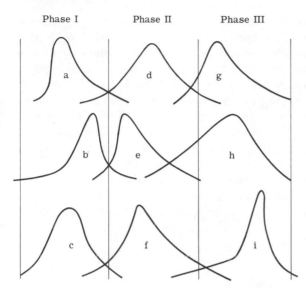

Figure 5.1. Phase definitions based on the
relative abundance of artifacts.

But, to arrange data in this fashion has a deleterious effect on an
investigator's ability to understand change: the two episodes of
change, from Phase I to II, and from Phase II to III, are obscured.
The changes fall half in one period and half in another. They are represented by the lines between the categories. Some investigators have
tried to circumvent this problem by creating chronologies focused on
changes, for example: incipient agriculture, developing agriculture,
and established agriculture. But, surely we hope to say more about
change than it starts to happen, it happens, it has happened.

Archeologists do sometimes use models that legitimately portray
changes in culture and behavior in a continuous fashion. Such is the
case, for example, when we construct a seriogram. But, we use
seriation for synchronic purposes—to date sites; and we do not see
the variability in behavior that is represented in such constructs. We
believe that changes in pottery styles over time approximate a normal
curve—a number of investigators using data of known dates, have
shown that such curves indeed have a normal, or "battleship," configuration. What we do not note is that the specific shape of such
curves varies considerably. Any innovation that has a beginning and
an end will have a battleship configuration, but some innovations are
adopted rapidly, others slowly; some achieve widespread use while

others do not; some are abandoned rapidly, others slowly. All of these factors produce curves that are highly variable in both length and width. If these curves are treated as records of variability in the adoption of innovations by human populations, they can be used in diachronic studies. However, they are usually used to date sites.

If an archeologist is willing to work toward the important contribution that our discipline can make to the understanding of behavioral and sociocultural changes, he must seek and use models that elucidate, rather than obscure, the patterns of change in the archeological record. Let us look briefly at the forms such models might take. I ask the reader to recognize that I have been heavily influenced by my own largely synchronic training. I intend these models as suggestions as to where we may wish to go, not as ultimately satisfactory models of change.

Behavioral Systems

Most archeological discussions of sociocultural phenomena are carried out today in a systems framework. Therefore, I will first examine a systems model. A system may be defined as two or more groups linked to each other by exchanges of matter and energy such that changes in one group will directly or indirectly produce changes in the other.

It is common in the anthropological literature to see a system discussed in analogy with a thermostat. This model is appropriate to only a very limited subset of systemic behavior. When the environment must be characterized in very amorphous terms and the signals that the population receives from the environment similarly treated,

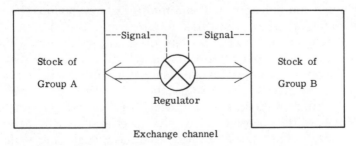

Figure 5.2. A systems model.

this model is appropriate. But many problems can be treated in terms of a far more bounded model of a system, which I will call the exchange model (see Figure 5.2). In this model two groups, A and B, each possess a stock of some resource. These stocks are linked by an exchange channel that may be either unidirectional or bidirectional; the channel has a regulator. In response to some signal from the environment, either A or B, or both, goods flow from one stock to another. (Clearly, we could construct a model that involved more groups and more exchange channels.) Thus, we could imagine that A and B possessed goods they had exchanged when one group's stock fell below some minimum. Or we might characterize an exchange of wives or information (reinforcement, affect, etc.).

The crucial condition that must characterize such a system under *stable environmental*[1] conditions is homeostasis. In simple terms, homeostatic conditions exist when the signal and the response are negatively correlated: A positive signal calls forth a negative flow and a negative signal calls forth a positive flow. Thus, in the illustration, a decrease in the stock of B would result in an increase in the flow. An increase in the stock would result in a decrease of the flow or even a reverse flow. Under these conditions, a constant level of a resource can be maintained in a stock.

Changes are occurring constantly in such situations. But the changes are deviation-countering changes. A deviation from the initial state evokes a response that returns the system to its original state.

The preceding discussion presumed that the system environment was characterized by normal fluctuations that did not exceed some limit or threshold. But there are conditions under which a change is so great that the response fails to restore the initial equilibrium. These conditions are called *environmental changes*, and the behavioral or sociocultural responses to them are called *morphogenic* or *deviation-amplifying*, changes. An action that was desirable in the past now creates problems, rather than affecting a solution.

For some systems and variables our knowledge of deviation-amplification is substantial. MacArthur and Connell (1966) have discussed the operation of population-regulating systems. Their analysis suggested that if the line corresponding to the ratio between

---

[1]Stability as used here does not imply invariance, but that key environmental variables show short-term fluctuations that do not exceed expected limits.

a change in population and the existing population ($dp : P$) is greater than 63°, equilibrium will never be restored. Every reaction will be an overreaction, until an entirely new equilibrium is established or the population in question ceases to exist.

Changes in a system environment that exceed established limits of variation are usually characterized as *stress*. It is not possible to predict by examining system components and their interaction when a stress will occur. That is, stress is an exogenous event. But when stress occurs, changes will probably be deviation-amplifying, rather than deviation-countering, and the system will either be replaced by a new one or the population will cease to exist.

In dealing with systems under changing and stable environmental conditions, one may distinguish two general classes of variables that measure system characteristics: *level variables* are measures of stocks of energy or information held by system components; *rate variables* are measures of changes in these stocks or in flows between specific system components. Level and rate variables may be used in constructing simulation models (see Zubrow 1971a,b), or in building time-trajectory models and studying the latter by formal or statistical techniques.

Systematic models are not useful for studying the whole range of sociocultural phenomena of interest to archeologists. In the first place, while it may be logically possible to build a model of a whole sociocultural system, the empirical work required to carry off such a task is mind-boggling, and there is some doubt that the result would be comprehensible. And yet, to compare systems using a system model, this is required. Second, it is questionable whether it is legitimate to use the term "adaptation" in speaking of systems. In the first place, this would not be a good analogy with the ecological literature, since in speaking of adaptation most ecologists would begin to discuss genes and gene flow. Moreover, the notion of a system adapting implies a rational determination of change and a decision to execute the change. While this does sometimes happen, it is more frequently the case that system change is a product of shifting behavior—some accidental, and some purposeful—of individuals within the system. Therefore, let us look at two other models, one focused on the problem of adaptation and the other focused on the problem of suprasystemic investigations.

Behavioral Strategies

Anthropologists are frequently concerned with the fashion in which individuals and groups accomplish particular ends. How do they acquire the food resources required for survival? How do they maintain equitable relationships between individuals? Alternatively, we are concerned with the why and wherefore of a particular item of behavior. Why do men give food to their mother's brother? Why do men in the society hunt rabbits? In asking such questions, we are implicitly or explicitly sensitive to other ways of behaving and other ways of accomplishing a given end that exist within that society or within other societies. It is the particular mixture of such alternatives that given individuals or groups practice that I have referred to as a strategy: a combination of two or more acts carried out by an individual that results in the acquisition of some natural or social resource. Alternative strategies are combinations of acts that result in the acquisition of the same natural or social resource.

Let us take as an example the subsistence practices of a population. At worst, anthropologists characterize a society as basically hunting and gathering or basically agricultural. At best, we may say that subsistence is derived 70% from the practice of agriculture and 30% from hunting and gathering. We should recognize that any individual in the population we are studying practices some combination of the two activities, and that the precise combination varies from individual to individual. At the community level, we also find variation in the average mix of the population of the community as an aggregate.

Thus, we may represent behavior that acquires some desired resources, in this case, subsistence resources, along a continuum, in this case, from hunting and gathering to agriculture. The variation along this continuum can be represented by a curve. (We will use a normal curve as a matter of convention, but no argument is made that all such distributions are normal ones.) Having represented behavioral variation in this fashion, we may begin to ask questions about the shape of the curve. Why does the curve have a given shape? Why does the mode occur at a particular point on the continuum? Why does the curve have a particular range of variation?

Answering these questions would force us to refer to processes, to linked series of events. It is argued that two processes underlie that shape of such a curve for a particular aggregate of individuals: variety-generation and selection.

Variety is continually generated in every human population. This variety exists in two forms. On the one hand, individuals *know how to accomplish* a given task in ways that are different from the ones they are actually practicing. On the other, there are individuals in the population who *are accomplishing* the same ends in different ways. That is to say, variety exists both in the minds of individuals who know of alternative behaviors but are not practicing them and in the actual practice of such strategies by deviant individuals within the population. This variety has a number of potential sources, including contact with other populations, mislearning, invention, and boredom. All of these act to generate variety within a population—to push the curve describing variations outward.

It is important to remember that one cannot predict what new item of behavior will be introduced into a society at a succeeding time period simply by looking at that society. Variety-generation is analogous to mutation in this regard. We can, however, make predictions about rates of variety-generation, rates of diffusion, and rates of innovation.

Clearly, variety-generation cannot be the only process that is operating in a system. If it were, the curve for most populations would tend to become infinitely broad or flat because the generation of variety tends to push the curve outward. The process that limits the generation of variety is referred to as *selection*. Selection produces both limits to the variety and a modal pattern of behavior.

Selective pressures emanate from the environment of the population. In speaking of selective pressures, we typically argue that the pattern of variation in behavior will closely reflect the variation in the environment, under stable conditions. A number of investigators in anthropology and other social sciences have argued that the modal pattern of behavior thus can be viewed. Sahlins and Service (1960:75), for example, have argued that the cultural system that is most effective in the exploitation of a given environment will spread at the expense of less effective systems. Homans (1970:36–37) has observed that, "When a response is followed by a reward, the frequence or probability of its recurrence increases." Sahlins and Service are discussing populations, and Homans is discussing individuals, but they concur in that there will be some strategy of behavior which is most common because it most effectively secures the social and natural resources, or rewards, of a given environment.

It is important that we carry the discussion of selection beyond this point, however, because selection is not only the cause of modal behavior, but also of limits. Behavior that does not secure any of the resources or rewards of a given situation will be dropped from the population's repertoire. But behavior that meets infrequently occurring environmental conditions will be retained, although to a minimal extent. Similarly, some variety will be created when resources necessary to practice the most desirable strategy are not available and alternatives must be sought.

To this point, the discussion of selection has been very abstract. It need not be left so—it is possible to specify both conscious and un-conscious, or mechanical, behavior that we can associate with selection. At the mechanical level, individuals within a population who are practicing inappropriate strategies will die or their offspring will die. Similarly, individuals who are practicing appropriate strate-gies will survive and produce viable offspring. At a conscious level, people are imitators; and if an individual notices someone down the road is securing more of a set of resources than he, he is likely to modify his behavior in that direction. Moreover, it may be desirable for the population as a whole to support individuals who in average years do poorly in securing necessary resources, but who are very pro-ductive in years when the environmental variable is tending toward its limit. Such individuals may represent the margin of survival for the population in difficult years.

Clearly, the curve for any population is a product of both variety-generating and selective pressures. If only variety-generation occurred, the curve would tend toward total flatness. If only selection occurred, the curve would tend toward total height, with no range at all. Neither condition occurs in nature, and variability described by some curve is the typical case. The interaction between variety-generation and selection is illustrated in Figure 5.3.

Processes of variety-generation and selection continue to operate under changing environmental conditions. In dealing with such situa-tions, the investigator must determine whether a given population or a given strategy is likely to survive in view of the environmental change that has occurred. It should be recalled that changing environment refers to a shift in both the mode of the environ-mental variable *and* its limits.

The most significant proposition put forth for making such a pre-diction is Sahlins and Service's (1960:97) law of evolutionary po-tential: "The more specialized and adapted a form in a given evolu-

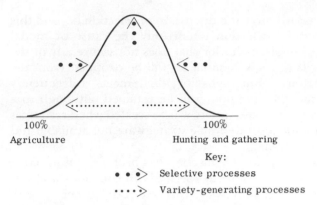

100%	100%
Agriculture	Hunting and gathering

Key:

● ● ●>   Selective processes

●●●●>   Variety-generating processes

Figure 5.3. The operation of variety and selection
on a subsistence strategy.

tionary stage, the smaller is its potential for passing to the next
stage." This proposition suffers from the evolutionary jargon in
which it is couched, and we may restate it to cover a broader range of
behavior as follows: The more specialized a population in acquiring
some resource, the lower the probability that the strategy will survive a change in some conditioning environmental variable; the less
specialized, the greater the probability. The vast literature in the
social sciences concerning the crucial role of marginal individuals in
periods of change becomes relevant when the proposition is formulated in this fashion. It is the presence of deviant individuals of different behavioral strategies that is important when environmental
change occurs.

We may see the validity of this proposition by returning to the
model of varying strategies used in considering the case of stable
environments. If a specialized population experiences an environmental change, it may not possess any individuals practicing strategies
appropriate to the changed conditions. If a diverse population
experiences a shift, there is a much higher probability that at least
some individuals in the population already will be practicing an
appropriate strategy. Their success under the new conditions will be
evident, as will the appropriate direction for behavioral modification.

Some qualifications must be put on such a model. First, the number
of individuals in the populations under consideration is a relevant
factor. If a highly varied population consists of only four individuals,
it is not likely that the population is going to survive, even given its
variety. If a more specialized population consists of thousands of

individuals, it will more probably survive than such a small one. The larger population lessens the risk of experimentation that follows a change.

The question of experimentation is itself important. There is some evidence to show that under stress conditions, experimentation increases. It is not evident at this point whether experimentation is increasing, or alternatives that had been only *known* are brought into *practice*. In any case, it is necessary to investigate the differential creativity of populations in responding to changes as a potentially important intervening variable.

In summary, we can surely say at this point that the probability of a population's continuing to practice a given strategy in the face of environmental change is directly proportional to both its size and diversity. Figure 5.4 illustrates the concepts used in studying strategies under changing conditions. The example is once again subsistence strategies and rainfall.

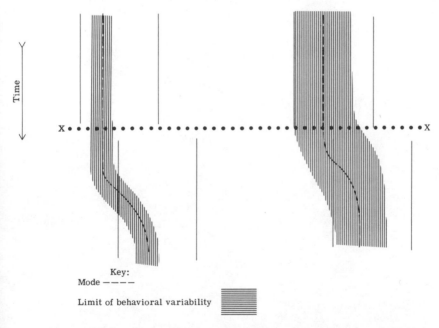

Figure 5.4. A model of the interaction of variety and selection. An environmental shift occurs at X. Some portion of the diversified population is already behaving in a fashion appropriate to the new conditions. The more specialized population experiences a period of time during which no one is behaving appropriately.

Dimensional or Dynamic-Equilibrium Models

At some point it becomes necessary for an investigator to deal with more than one sociocultural system. Therefore, it is imperative that he have some notion of the most important or basic characteristics of cultural systems. I call such characteristics, dimensions. The analogy is to dimensions in the natural sciences since these are never causally related to each other—space does not cause time. Nevertheless, I will use the term in reference to basic categories, each of which includes a set of commonly used variables that are essentially varied modifications of a single data base or observational set.

I will discuss these in a separate chapter for two reasons. First, such models were the basis of my doctoral dissertation, and I have a great deal more experience in defining and using them. Second, of the three kinds of models I have discussed, they seem most applicable to archeological data and most appropriate to diachronic analyses.

CHAPTER SIX

A Dimensional
or Dynamic-Equilibrium
Model of Change

In constructing this model of change, I will rely heavily on data that describes processes of growth in the developing nations of the modern world. I do so because *some* such studies have in fact employed diachronic data and because this literature contains many precise statements or hypotheses and a rich literature that describes change. The kinds of changes associated with development in the modern world are usually referred to as growth. Miller (1965a:372) defines growth as follows:

> [Growth is] . . . a progressive, developmental matter–energy process which occurs at all levels of systems, [which] involves (a) increase in size . . . of the system, and commonly also (b) rise in the number of components of it; (c) increase in its complexity; (d) reorganization of relationships among its structures . . . and their processes, including differentiation of specialized structures and patterns of action; and (e) increase in the amounts of matter energy and information it processes.

Miller is discussing systems in general, and not cultural systems. Nevertheless, there is a fundamental similarity between his definition and the dimensions that have concerned anthropologists in their analyses of growth. Leslie White (1959:293) examines the Neolithic of the Near East and finds the following basic changes:

> (1) Agriculture and animal husbandry made possible increased food production both (a) per acre and (b) per man-hour. (2) Pressure of population increase brought about increased food production, which in turn tended toward further growth of population. (3) The productivity of labor, i.e., amount of food per man-hour, increased as the agricultural arts and those of animal husbandry were developed. (4) As the density of population increased, society became more structurally differentiated and functionally specialized; i.e., a portion of the productive members of society were divorced from food getting and their time and labor were devoted to various arts and crafts.... (5) The developments made a change of economic system necessary. (6) Concomitantly with the growth of population in size and density and concomitantly with the structural differentiation and functional specialization of society, there was developed a special political mechanism, the state-church.... (7) The result was a division of society into a dominant, ruling class and a subordinate class.

White is contrasting hunting and gathering and agricultural cultures at a very abstract level. His conclusions suggest that critical differences between these levels of organization might be viewed as the kind of change that Miller calls growth.

Modern analyses of growth lead to an essentially similar conclusion concerning its dimensions of variability. Berry (1961) and Adelman and Morris (1967) have performed factor analyses on over 50 cultural and technological indices of industrialization. They conclude that only a few patterns or dimensions of variability underlie these many variables. These dimensions are similar to those discussed by Miller and White. I believe that the insights provided by Miller (1965a,b), White (1959), Adelman and Morris (1967), and Berry (1961) suggest four primary dimensions of variability in processes of growth: population, differentiation, integration, and energy or resources. A model focusing on these four dimensions will be constructed.

Before going into the details of this model, several of its more implicit aspects must be made clear. First, I have assumed that processes of growth have a nonrandom distribution in time and space: Growth does not occur at an even rate at all times and in all places. For any living system there are periods of growth and periods of nongrowth. Gellner (1964:43) finds it useful,

> ... to view history as a succession of plateaux, interrupted by steep, near perpendicular cliffs by the dramatic and profound transformations. There was the neolithic revolution and there is the industrial one, and the sociology of either must be concerned primarily with change. . . .

This view of growth has been embraced by Parsons and Smelser (1956:179), Rostow (1960:7), and Miller (1965a).

Second, the model initially will be bivariate, in that it is based upon relationships between linked pairs of variables. This does not mean that multivariate combinations do not exist. If they do, then links between pairs of variables must underly their existence. The model, then, will be a simple one that seeks to understand the fundamental linkages and not one that supplies multivariate paths through a matrix.

The model is more "ideal" than "real." It is ideal in the sense that *ceterus paribus* is invoked throughout. That is, when any statement is made concerning the relationships between two variables or dimensions, I am assuming that all other things are equal; the potential interference from unmeasured variability is held constant. This assumption is particularly crucial to the use of the term "sufficient" in the argument that follows.

Finally, the "conclusions" of the analysis must be understood as hypotheses. I do not intend that they be interpreted as statements of fact, empirical generalizations, or laws, but only as hypotheses derived from the examination of a single case of growth. Having set forth these qualifications, I will not repeat them in the specific cases where they apply.

A Model of Growth

The model of growth followed here focuses on four dimensions: population, differentiation, integration, and energy. These dimensions were defined simply in Miller's definition of growth: Population is the size of a system, differentiation is the number of parts, integration is the strength of ties between parts, and energy is the quantity of resources the system is processing.

We may gain a somewhat more precise definition of these dimensions by examining some variables that are relevant to each.

1. Population
   a. Population is the number of individuals in a given area at a given time.
   b. Population growth is the increase over a specified time period in the number of individuals in a given area.
   c. The age composition of a population is the distributional curve of the ages of the aggregate of individuals inhabiting a given area at a given time.
   d. Density is the number of individuals per unit area.
   e. Potential of population is the number of individuals per unit distance.
2. Differentiation
   a. Differentiation is the number of different activities performed in a given place at a given time.
   b. Specialization is a measure of differences in magnitude and discreteness of different activities within the aggregate.
   c. Individual specialization is the percentage of activities that a given individual performs relative to the aggregate of activities performed by the group of which he is a member.
3. Integration
   a. Integration concerns the degree of definition and mutual recognition of roles that coordinate a set of activities.
   b. Integration concerns the degree of acceptance of institutions that coordinate a set of activities.
   c. Integration concerns the sharedness of symbols that coordinate a set of activities.
4. Energy
   a. Energy is the gross quantity of energy produced and used by the inhabitants of a given region during a given period of time.
   b. Productivity is the output of energy per unit input of labor produced by the inhabitants of a given region during a given period of time.
   c. Environmental potential is a measure of the productive potential of a given plant–animal community for exploitation at a given level of technology.

This list of variables by no means exhausts the possibilities for measuring each dimension. It does represent frequently used variables for each dimension.

Constructing a model of growth requires determining the significant causal relationships between each of the four dimensions. Since change in any one dimension could conceivably account for change in any other, there are 16 potentially significant relationships between paired variables. These relationships are represented in Table 6.1. Table 6.1 is read as follows: The row *(x)* dimensions are considered as possible conditions for change in the column *(y)* dimensions. To read across a row is to ask, given that changes are occurring in *x* what changes in *y* will also occur? For example, given that changes are

TABLE 6.1
Matrix of Logically Possible Relationships
between Changes in the Four Dimensions

Independent dimension (x)	Dependent dimension (y)			
	Population	Differentiation	Integration	Energy
Population	A change in population is a sufficient condition for a change in population.	A change in population is a sufficient condition for a change in differentiation.	A change in population is a sufficient condition for a change in integration.	A change in population is a sufficient condition for a change in energy.
Differentiation	A change in differentiation is a sufficient condition for a change in population.	A change in differentiation is a sufficient condition for a change in differentiation.	A change in differentiation is a sufficient condition for a change in integration.	A change in differentiation is a sufficient condition for a change in energy.
Integration	A change in integration is a sufficient condition for a change in population.	A change in integration is a sufficient condition for a change in differentiation.	A change in integration is a sufficient condition for a change in integration.	A change in integration is a sufficient condition for a change in energy.
Energy	A change in energy is a sufficient condition for a change in population.	A change in energy is a sufficient condition for a change in differentiation.	A change in energy is a sufficient condition for a change in integration.	A change in energy is a sufficient condition for a change in energy.

occurring in population, what changes are occurring in differentiation, integration, and energy? To read down a column is to ask what changes in a column (y) dimensions can be accounted for by changes in the row (x) dimensions. For example, what changes in population (Column 1) can be accounted for by changes in differentiation, integration, and energy.

In Table 6.1 there are 16 statements that describe each of the possible relationships between dimensions. Four of these can be excluded at the outset. The purpose of the analysis is to discover meaningful relationships between dimensions. Each of these cells contains a statement in which a dimension is identified as the cause for changes in itself. Given the conditions defined for the model, such statements are meaningless. Therefore, I will ignore the statements in these 4 cells and limit further consideration to the remaining 12 cells in the matrix.

The relationships defined in Table 6.1 are logically possible. It must be determined which of these are *more* than logically possible and seem to account for changes that occur in the real world. To make this determination, I will search the literature of industrialization, analyzing the matrix one column at a time, and attempting to explain changes in each of the dimensions by arguments that link changes in it with changes in the other dimensions.

POPULATION

Relationships in the matrix that could account for changes in population are the following:

A change in differentiation is a sufficient condition for a change in population.

A change in integration is a sufficient condition for a change in population.

A change in energy is a sufficient condition for a change in population.

Virtually every author who has studied the process of industrialization in the present or in the past has noted that countries experiencing industrialization experience changes in rates of population increase. These authors often divide population growth into two periods (see Davis 1963): In the first period, the rate of population growth increases; in the second, the rate slows until a relatively low and quite stable rate of increase is achieved. While rates of growth have varied, increases in the rates have affected almost every country that has experienced industrialization (Clark 1967; Davis 1963:69).

The initial increase in population is generally attributed to a decline in death rates while birth rates remain constant (Clark 1967; Davis 1963:64; Davis and Blake 1956; Rostow 1960:140). Two factors have been associated with the decrease in death rates. (1) The decrease has been attributed to an increase in medical knowledge. Longevity increases, but there is no offsetting effect on birth rates. (2) It has also been attributed to a general rise in the standard of living: improved food, clothing, housing, and sanitation.

There has been considerable argument over which of these two explanations is correct (Davis 1963:70). I see no need to view them as mutually exclusive. Increases in medical knowledge and increases in the standard of living are both changes associated with the dimension of energy or resources. Some investigators stress resources as know-how, medical knowledge. Others stress resources in concrete form— food, clothing, and housing. One would expect a correspondence between increases in know-how and increases in the standard of living writ large. Both increase longevity, and neither has an effect that reduces fertility. In the absence of some stimulus to a reduction of fertility, an increase in technological effectiveness is a sufficient condition for an increase in population.

The change in growth rates in the developmental process also results from a second effect of energy on population. Myrdal (1957: 23–24), Hirschmann (1958:188), and other analysts (see Baer 1964; Lausen 1962), have argued that population tends to flow from lagging to leading areas. The flow represents a preference for a higher or more secure standard of living, or at least the possibility of a higher standard of living. Areas that are already successfully manipulating energy grow at the expense of areas that are not so successful. Not all regions are equally successful in producing energy, and population tends to flow from less successful regions to those that are more so.

An immediate effect of the migration is a reduction in the population of donor areas. Within a region, population concentrates in a few subregions. Within a subregion, population becomes increasingly concentrated in a few communities. Thus, population growth with industrialization is associated with increasing concentration of population, i.e., urbanization (Davis 1963:71; Davis and Golden 1954; Hauser 1964; Lampard 1954; Mabogunje 1964).

Although migration has the immediate effect of increasing the population of recipient areas, it has the long-term effect of slowing the increase. Several observers have noted that rates of population increase are lower in urban, than in rural, areas. Stewart and Warntz (1967:136) have analyzed 412 cities in the United States and shown that as the potential of population (population per unit of distance) increases, the excess of births over deaths decreases. Clark (1967) has summarized more than a dozen national studies that show this same phenomenon. The most frequent explanation of it associates dense populations with an increased rate of transmission of diseases due to sanitation and nutrition problems (Davis 1963:63; Polgar 1964: 206–207; Sigerist 1943; Wynne-Edwards 1962). Moreover, one would expect that devices of population control will be instituted as the carrying capacity limit is approached. In short, increasing density results in a decrease in the rate of population growth.

I have associated changes in population with changes in resources and present the following hypotheses:

1. A change in resources is a sufficient condition for a change in population.
   a. Increasing standards of nutrition and technical know-how cause increasing fertility and increasing longevity.
   b. If increasing energy is based on differentially distributed resources: (1) population flows from lagging to leading areas and becomes more densely concentrated in a few centers; (2) increasing density causes a decline in the rate of growth because increasing density is associated with problems of disease and nutrition.

DIFFERENTIATION

Differentiation in a general sense refers to evolution from multifunctional role structures to more specialized ones (Smelser 1963: 106). Industrialization has been associated with differentiation in the social and the economic sphere. Adelman and Morris (1967:206) argue that "one may look at the entire process of national modernization as the progressive differentiation of the social, economic and political sphere from each other and the development of specialized institutions in each sphere." Activities are broken into finer and finer units and the role the individual plays in the aggregate of activities is diminished.

Processes of differentiation are at work in the family and in society at large, in economic and in noneconomic spheres. Smelser (1963) has summarized the role of differentiation in industrialization as follows:

> (1) In the transition from domestic to factory industry, the division of labor increases, and the economic activities previously lodged in the family move to the factory. (2) With the rise of a formal educational system the training functions previously performed in large part by the family and church are established in a more specialized unit, the school. (3) The modern political party has a more complex structure than tribal factions [p. 106].

Smelser lists a number of specific changes that are associated with the dimension of differentiation.

1. Economic activities
   a. The introduction of money crops differentiates the social contexts of production and consumption.
   b. Wage labor undermines the family production unit.
   c. Household industry is replaced by the factory system that separates the worker from both family and capital.
   d. More and more goods and services are exchanged in the market.
2. Differentiation of family activities
   a. Apprenticeship within the family declines.
   b. Pressures develop against the intervention of family favoritism in the recruitment of labor and management.
   c. The direct controls of elder and collateral kinsmen over the nuclear family weakens.

Similar arguments for the particular case of Africa are given by Dalton (1964).

An explanation for the association of differentiation and industrialization was offered by Durkheim. Durkheim (1964:262) argued:

> The division of labor varies in direct ratio with the volume and density of societies, and if it progresses in a continuous manner in the course of social development, it is because societies become regularly denser and more voluminous.

Durkheim believed that with an increasing number of people and increasing mutual proximity of the people, the quantity of social contact would increase markedly. This, he believed, would result in uncontrollable conflict between individuals if the individuals in question were pursuing similar goals. Functional differentiation is a means of reducing conflict in a population that is both growing and becoming denser.

Park (1950), Lampard (1954), and White (1959:293) have all argued that density is a basic cause of differentiation. All point to the need for a large proximous population if differentiation is to occur. Clark (1967) and Hagen (in Clark 1967) have argued that increasing density results in economies of scale. Such an argument leaves out the intermediate step of differentiation in relating population and technology, but underscores the basic causal dimension, population.

An independent argument based on age composition links differentiation and population in a second manner. James G. Miller (1965b: 384) has proposed a cross-level hypothesis to the effect that increasing differentiation occurs as a product of increasing longevity. "The more rapid the reassignment of function from one component to another a long surviving system has, the more likely are the components to be totipotential rather than partipotential." This hypothesis originated from studies of the organization of the United States Army. The observations of differentiation in the army indicated that because there are few individuals who remain in the army for their entire life and because the risk of death is high, the army trains few specialists. Most soldiers are trained to be competent in a variety of different activities. Neither the returns for energy expended in training that are lost when an individual leaves the service, nor the risk of death in warfare, make specialization feasible.

The relationships that characterize army organization can be applied to human groups in general. In a society with a low life expectancy, with a high mortality rate in all age groups, it is impossible to train specialists: The risk is too high. But when a population achieves greater longevity, and when these longer-living individuals are close to each other, the replacement of a specialist who dies or leaves the system is possible—thus, specialization is possible.

Changes in differentiation are also caused by changes in the resource dimension. Changes in the loci of resources being utilized by an adaptation and experimentation with new resources may account for changes in differentiation. Haggett (1966:95) has discussed the effect of differentially distributed resources on settlement pattern. Dalton (1964) has shown the effect of factories on a culture that formerly relied on localized sources for energy and tools. In short, a culture that relies upon, or is experimenting with, many different energy sources will be more differentiated than one that relies on only a few. And the greater the spatial separation of these resources, the greater the differentiation.

The view of the dimension of differentiation that I have advanced links changes in differentiation with changes in technology and population. Increasing population, increasing density, and increasing longevity warrant organizational changes that reduce individual conflicts in activity performance. Finally, increasing longevity is necessary in order to make a specialized organization a viable one. Differentiation also changes in response to the number and geographical distribution of energy sources. The following hypotheses result from this analysis.

1. A change in population is a sufficient condition for a change in differentiation.
   a. Increasing density causes increasing differentiation.
   b. Increasing longevity causes increasing differentiation.
2. A change in technology is a sufficient condition for a change in differentiation.
   a. Increasing numbers of energy sources cause increasing differentiation.
   b. Increasing geographical discreteness of energy causes increasing differentiation.

INTEGRATION

In recent years, attention has been given to the roles of integrative symbols, roles, and institutions in industrialization. Some complexes of these variables have been identified as conducive to growth, others as barriers. Nash (1958) has presented a detailed list of the manner in which different values and institutions promote or inhibit growth. McClelland (1964) has analyzed problems of industrialization in terms of achievement motivation. Hagen (1964) sees the transition as a question of replacing a traditional elite with a modern one. Adelman and Morris (1967) find that particular changes within the overall transition are responses to the institutional and value structures of Western capitalism. A host of other authors have argued that particular sets of values must change if growth is to be successful (Dalton 1964; Eckstein 1957; Hauser 1964; Hoselitz 1954; Lambert 1964; Lampard 1954; Myrdal 1955; Shils 1964; Tumin 1964).

The basic insight into the kinds of changes in integrative variables that promote growth were again set forth by Durkheim. If a differentiating society is to remain viable, differentiation cannot proceed beyond some point where interaction between individuals ceases. Differentiation is an integral part of growth. Uncontrolled differentiation results in the dissolution of the system in which it is occurring. An initial contrapuntal force to increasing differentiation is the relationship between individual roles and independence. As an individual plays an increasingly smaller role in the aggregate of productive processes, he becomes more dependent upon others for an increasingly large portion of his livelihood. Thus, differentiation results in a greater dependence of individuals upon each other for their mutual welfare (Davis and Golden 1954:23; Hauser 1964:248; Lampard 1954:90–91; Levy 1966:49).

Changes in integration are seen as results of changes in differentiation. As economic activities are differentiated, the individual plays a smaller role in producing his own livelihood, and is more dependent upon his fellows. At the same time, the integrative system itself is undergoing processes of differentiation: Specialized roles and institutions result. So close is the relationship between differentiation and integration that some analysts have argued that a measurement of changes in differentiation also measures changes in integration (Young and Fujimoto, 1965:350–351).

The following hypotheses are suggested by this analysis. A change in differentiation is a sufficient condition for a change in integration.

1. Increasing differentiation is a sufficient condition for increasing mutual dependency of individuals and groups.
2. Increasing differentiation is a sufficient condition for increasing role specialization in integrative sphere.
3. Increasing differentiation is a sufficient condition for increasing specialization in integrative institutions.

ENERGY

An analysis of the literature of industrialization suggests that a change in any of the other dimensions is a sufficient condition for a change in resources. The relationships between differentiation and energy and integration and energy are straightforward, and I will discuss them first. The relation of population change to changes in energy, which is more complex, will be discussed last and in greater detail.

A change in differentiation is a sufficient condition for a change in energy. The argument for this hypothesis is very old. It was originally formulated by Adam Smith in the *Wealth of Nations*. One man can make a few dozen pins on a given day. But a group of men, sub-divided with respect to function in such a way that each performs a single operation over and over can turn out a far greater number of pins in the same time. Simple, repetitive acts are more productive than complex ones and result in greater outputs of energy per unit of input.

Two other increments to energy result from differentiation. When an individual concentrates on a single task, he is more likely to be-come skilled in the performance of that task than he would if it were only one of a number of tasks he performed. Second, when division of labor exists, no one member of an organization is required to possess all of the technology used in the aggregate of activities carried on by the society. That is, the need for tools is relatively less under conditions of differentiation.

A change in integration is a sufficient condition for a change in energy. A well-integrated system performs any task more efficiently than a poorly integrated one. The less overlap of function and the fewer deviations from norms, the less energy is expended in "noise," in unproductive activities.

The role changes in population play in changes in energy is the sub-ject of much argument—completely conflicting viewpoints have been advanced. One group of investigators suggests that population in-creases are the primary cause of innovation and increases in energy production. A second group argues that population increases are the primary barriers to increases in energy production.

The primary advocate of the causal role of population in industri-alization is Colin Clark. Clark (1967:134) argues that:

> In the great majority of cases, it is population change which is the cause and technical and political change the consequence ... it is very unlikely that any people should of their own initiative institute changes in agricultural technique. ... They would only initiate such changes when compelled to do so by increasing population pressure.

Clark sees population's positive effect on energy in four areas. (1) Individuals always fight to retain an already achieved standard of living. Population pressure threatens the existing standard of living. Attempts to return to a standard of living threatened by population increases lead not to a simple maintenance of the old standard, but to structural changes that result in a higher one (Clark 1967:134; Hirschmann 1958:177). (2) A growing population implies a distribution of risk over a greater number of heads. Given that technological innovations involve risk—perhaps with potential threats to the survival of an adaptation—risks are easier to bear with a large and growing population (Clark 1967:255; Hagen, cited in Clark 1967:256; Spengler 1961:254). (3) With a large population, economies of scale that are not possible with small populations become possible. This is especially true of public works (Hagen, cited in Clark 1967:255; Klieman 1966:40–44). (4) Population growth leads to increased savings. The proportion of old people, who are consumers not savers, is reduced in a growing population. Furthermore, large families save more than do small families (Clark 1967:267). Boserup (1969) has expanded on many of Clark's arguments.

The absolute level of a population, its density, its rate of growth, and its age composition are critical in Clark's analysis. Each of these variables is held to have a positive correlation with changes in energy production.

Davis (1968) has responded directly to each of Clark's points and challenged the validity of his analysis. (1) To argue that population pressure is advantageous because the response to it is beneficial is to justify any form of hardship (p. 134). (2) There is no correlation between population growth and capital formation (p. 134). (3) There is no correlation between population growth and growth associated with economies of scale (p. 135). (4) The primary effect of changes in age composition is deleterious to savings. Rapid population increases result in an increase in very young and very old age groups. The ratio of nonproducers to producers increases and output per capita falls (p. 133; see also Coale 1963:47; Kamerschen 1965:182; and Spengler 1961:252).

Most students of industrialization would tend to support the views set forth by Davis rather than those of Clark. By far the most damaging blows to Clark's position derive from the many attempts to correlate population change and change in various indicators of energy production. Clark acknowledges Kuznet's failure to find the predicted correlations; Davis uses Clark's data to show that no correlations exist; and many other economists have pointed to similar noncorrelations. Frederiksen (1966), for example, has analyzed decennial change in product per capita, animal protein per capita, newsprint consumption, and physicians per 1000 persons for 21 countries. His analysis indicates a slight and generally negative correlation among these variables and a set that measures population growth.

Clark presents and justifies a series of theoretical arguments suggesting that population increases ought to have a positive effect on technology. Statistics from industrializing nations today, as well as from historical cases, do not support his predictions. In short, Clark's ideas lead to an absurd conclusion: The best way to promote development in the underdeveloped world is to promote population growth. By promoting hardship, we will provoke a response that will improve the standard of living of such areas. Clearly, Clark's ideas are not very helpful in solving problems of the industrializing world.

It is not, however, necessary to throw out all of Clark's analysis. Davis (1968:134) points out that some of Clark's arguments that are not valid in the modern world are valid in frontier societies where migration is possible. Thus, when the age composition of a population can be regulated, it is possible that an increase in population will lead to an increase in energy. When the increase does not occur at the expense of producers, energy is in fact increased.

Additionally, Clark's ideas apply to gross systemic changes over large periods of time, while most of his critics are interested in planning specific changes over shorter periods of time. Since Clark's greatest critic has suggested that his arguments may hold under conditions that are similar to prehistoric ones, and since his arguments apply to long-term change at a systemic level, they may offer insight into prehistoric change even though they are not useful in development planning. At least, it would be intellectually dishonest to not consider them as hypotheses.

Changes in energy may occur as the result of changes in any of the other dimensions. Specifically:

1. A change in differentiation is a sufficient condition for a change in output per unit input.
2. A change in integration is a sufficient condition for a change in efficiency.
3. A change in population is a sufficient condition for a change in energy production.

Recapitulation

The purpose of this analysis has been to gain some insight into the dimensions of variability that have been found useful in analyzing industrialization. These insights are taken as suggestions as to what variables might be important in explaining another transformation—the agricultural revolution. While some of the analysis has touched upon variables drawn from formal economic models, its concern is not with such formal models. The analysis seeks insight into important relationships; it does not seek to apply formal economic models useful in industrialization to explain prehistoric economic transformations.

The analysis focused upon 12 potentially meaningful relationships among 4 dimensions. Seven of these relationships seem to be meaningful ones; these are stated in Table 6.2, a matrix that has been revised from Table 6.1. A change in any one dimension is not directly responsible for changes in all the other dimensions—but, indirectly (*a* causes change in *b*, *b* causes change in *c*) a change in any one dimension leads to changes in each of the others.

Almost 200 test implications result from the permutation of variables used in measuring each dimension. There are, then, many possible tests of the model. Our purpose in Chapter 7 will be to apply the model to the case of technological change and to identify test implications of the model that can be handled in a prehistoric context.

It should be noted that the discussion of growth to this point has focused on growth rather than nongrowth. Ultimately, in order to understand change, we must be as concerned with nongrowth as with growth. However, since the social science literature dealing with growth largely focuses on the current conditions of growth in nations undergoing change, we know very little about nongrowth. It is hoped that by the end of this work we will be able to make some preliminary suggestions as to the nature of nongrowth.

Technology

The relationship of this model to technology has been defined to some extent by specific references to technological changes in discussions of relationships among the various dimensions. Since, however, the existing definition of the Basketmaker–Pueblo transi-

TABLE 6.2
Matrix of Probable Relationships between Changes in the Four Dimensions

Independent dimension (x)	Dependent dimension (y)			
	Population	Differentiation	Integration	Energy
Population		A change in population is a sufficient condition for a change in differentiation.		A change in population is a sufficient condition for a change in energy.
Differentiation			A change in differentiation is a sufficient condition for a change in integration.	A change in differentiation is a sufficient condition for a change in energy.
Integration				A change in integration is a sufficient condition for a change in energy.
Energy	A change in energy is a sufficient condition for a change in population.	A change in technology is a sufficient condition for a change in differentiation.		

tion is stated in technological terms, it is appropriate to develop somewhat more fully the concept of technological change that is employed in this study and to specify the relationship between technological change and change in each of the dimensions—population, differentiation, integration, and energy.

The technological changes that characterize the Basketmaker–Pueblo transition involve, primarily, technomic rather than ideotechnic or sociotechnic artifacts. I view the set of technomic artifacts that any society possesses as a strategy. Tools stand in complementary and competing relationships with each other. For the case of technomic artifacts, the strategy, the technological strategy that characterizes a given society, must be adapted to the tasks of acquiring and processing subsistence and maintenance resources within the local environment. Consistent with the discussion of strategy in Chapter 5, one expects that tool kits will vary among individuals, households, and communities. But, for any household, community, or society, one can characterize an average tool kit composed of different kinds of artifacts and different relative frequencies of given kinds of artifacts, which represents the technological strategy practiced by the group in question. Over time, changes in the technological strategy of the group will be observed as changes in the kinds of tools and relative frequencies of tools represented. Just as we may investigate the kinds of tools that exist in a specific tool kit, we may also ask questions that pertain to the tools as groups: how efficient is the process of making the tools, how efficient is the process of using the tools, etc.

In that we have identified the organization of a society's maintenance and subsistence activities as the primary factors that shape the technological strategy, we would expect the principle dimension causing technological change to be differentiation. On the one hand, the more specialized the activity structure of the society, the more specialized and complex the average tool kit that we would expect to find in that society. On the other, for the reasons outlined earlier, we expect that differentiation and specialization will lead to increasing efficiency in processes of tool manufacture and tool use.

However, we can identify causal and facilitative relationships between changes in each of the other dimensions and technological change. In the case of population, arguments were cited to the effect that the larger the number of individuals in a population, the less the risk of innovation. We might also note that with larger numbers of individuals by random processes alone we would expect to find more ideas about tools and technological strategies and, therefore, a larger pool of innovations upon which selective pressures may operate. Similarly, different integrative mechanisms may lead to smaller or larger pools of variety and may facilitate or hinder the sharing of these ideas within a given population. The number of different energy sources that a population is exploiting, quite apart from the specific differentiation of exploitative activities, will affect the technological strategy, as will the appearance of new energy resources.

These closing comments are intended as a summary of the relationship between technology and the other dimensions. More specific information on these relationships may be found in the discussions of each of the dimensions. The point of this analysis is simple: All of the dimensions may have an impact on technological change, but we should expect changes in the dimension of differentiation to have the greatest impact. Similarly, to the extent that exogenous technological changes may have an impact on the other dimensions, we should expect such changes to be reflected in a change in differentiation.

CHAPTER SEVEN

Test Implications

Two sets of ideas concerning the problem at hand have been developed. First, the changes that occurred during the period A.D. 500–1000 in the prehistoric Southwest and hypotheses concerning their probable causes have been discussed. Second, a model that isolates the major dimensions of variability (population, differentiation, integration, and energy) used by social scientists in studying industrialization has been presented. This chapter ties these two sets of ideas together in the form of test implications—predictions of what configuration specific classes of data must take if the kinds of variability that explain processes of industrialization can be used to form a model that explains the technological changes of the Basketmaker–Pueblo transition.

The primary problem in this regard was the selection of prehistoric variables that measure the four dimensions of variability. In defining and discussing each of these dimensions, a long list of types of variables used in modern analyses was presented. At first glance, it might seem impossible that similar variables could be used in prehistoric situations. For each of the dimensions, archeologists not only can use, but have used, variables that are counterparts of those used in analysis of the present. Furthermore, in the following chapters, I will present arguments of relevance—reasons why these variables accurately measure changes in the relevant dimension.

Archeological Research and the Dimensions

Creighton Gabel's (1967) *Analysis of Prehistoric Economic Patterns* provides a starting point in discussing the relationship between archeological research and the dimensions. Gabel divides the book into chapters that focus on the food quest (including sources of food, production, seasonal cycles, storage, and food intake), land use, demography, raw materials, crafts, and labor (including the division of labor), trade, reciprocity, and redistribution. He suggests how, where, and when archeologists have considered these topics in discussing economic patterns in prehistory.

There are close parallels between Gabel's chapter topics and the dimensions that I have suggested underlie the many analyses of industrialization. His demography topic and the dimension of population are identical. His concern with land use and with production, seasonal cycles, crafts, labor, and the division of labor closely parallel the kinds of issues examined by analysts concerned with what I have labeled differentiation. Integration as a dimension would encompass the topics with which Gabel is concerned in his discussion of trade, reciprocity, and redistribution. Finally, a study of the dimension of energy includes studies of raw materials, storage, and food intake.

Gabel discusses a number of works by archeologists in which these specific topics have been examined. Archeologists have been, and are, interested in the analysis of variables that measure the same four dimensions measured by students of industrialization. What divides the archeologists and students of modern human populations are the data with which they work and the operational variables they use. In terms of the dimensions along which they explain patterns of change, there is a fundamental similarity.

By the same token, the novelty in the point of view I am taking does not lie at the level of suggesting that archeologists should become concerned with a set of variables with which they have previously been unconcerned. All the variables that will be used have been used before. What is novel about the approach taken here is the attempt to see interrelationships between the dimensions and between variables and the application of rigorous techniques of measurement. Too often the measurement of one dimension or variable is an end in itself. One writes an article on population, for example; one identifies changes; there the analysis stops (cf. Eddy 1966; Hayes 1964; Schwartz 1956). If we are going to take the time to measure variables that are rather difficult to measure, then we ought to devote attention to explaining why they vary. If population is a subject archeologists should study, and if there are demographic variables that should be quantified, then population and variables measuring it should be understood and explained.

Test Implications

Testing the explanatory worth of the model involves finding variables that measure variability in each dimension, and determining precisely how these variables should vary, and whether they can be used to predict the changes associated with the Basketmaker–Pueblo transition. Since the transition from Basketmaker is an apparent instance of positive, rather than negative, growth, the dimensions should vary together in a positive fashion. That is population, differentiation, and technology should increase, and integrative mechanisms become more complex or effective. What variables measure changes in each of these dimensions? How should they vary if the four dimensions have a positive relationship with each other? How should they vary if the arguments as to why the relationships between dimensions exist are correct? If the transition from Basketmaker to Pueblo culture is in fact economic, and if the model in fact explains the changes that occurred, then for any data that might be examined, the following changes should be coincidental with the transformation.

POPULATION

If the model has explanatory power, changes in the dimension of population ought to occur during the transition. The prehistoric population of a region is reflected in the *number of dwelling units* that are inhabited at a given point in time. The more dwelling units, the greater is the population. The number of dwelling units should increase rapidly during the transition. This prediction will be deemed accurate if the increase in population is as rapid or more rapid than any other increase in the local culture history and if the increase results in a population maximum for the region. Requiring changes in both the rate and absolute level is simply an attempt to be certain that a significant change in the dimension of population is occurring.

During a transition, the distribution of population should also change; it should become more dense. Population should begin to concentrate in areas that are most efficient in exploiting energy. Moreover, increases in population density are critical to the model because such changes have been postulated as a major link between changes in the dimensions of population and differentiation. Thus, on the basis of the model, density ought to increase and reach a maximum. For prehistoric populations, density can be measured by examining the *number of sites per square mile, the mean distance between sites, and the nearest neighbor distribution of sites.* To the extent that these variables reflect changes in the dimension of population and to the extent that the dimension is changing, the variables should change both in rate and in level. Again, predicting both absolute and relative change is a means of insuring that significant change is occurring.

DIFFERENTIATION

Changes in the locus and organization of activities ought to occur if the model accurately explains economic transformations. Such changes are caused by changes in density and changes in the distribution of resources. Evidence of change in the dimension of differentiation should exist both within and between sites.

One measure of changes in differentiation is the number of *different kinds of activity sites.* The differentiation of activities, were it occurring, might be reflected in the arrangement of activities on sites. The more kinds of sites with distinctive activities, the more differentiated is the total activity process. The significance of changes in the presence of limited-activity sites may be evaluated by looking at both rate and level. The proposition that activities are becoming more differentiated on an intersite basis will be accepted if the total area of limited-activity sites increases at its most rapid rate and reaches a maximum during the transition; and if the coefficient of variability analysis indicates there is a tendency for more types of limited-activity sites to be present during this period than during any other. The relationship between any pattern of change in differentiation of activities and changes in the location of resources may be analyzed by noting the location of the sites. Again, if diversification in activities is associated with resource changes, then *diversity in the use of resources, that is, experimenta-*

tion, in the location of sites, ought to reach a maximum at the same time that differentiation does.

Within sites, the model suggests that activity space ought to become more differentiated. Operationally, it ought to become more specialized. Because specialization is difficult to measure, some of the consideration of differentiation within sites will be purely descriptive. At a more concrete level, the kinds of artifacts that are used in a given quantity of space provide an indication of the degree of specialization of that space. Specialized space should contain artifactual evidence that one activity or a limited range of activities was performed there. Generalized space should contain evidence of a variety of activities. For dwelling units, Pueblo sites should have greater *room-to-room variability in artifacts* than Basketmaker sites. Such a distribution would indicate that different rooms were being used for different activities. A coefficient of variability for a series of Pueblo dwelling units might be higher than one for Basketmaker units.

This same principle can be applied to outdoor space. There might be more squares containing only a single artifact type in Pueblo than in Basketmaker sites. In general, the kinds of artifacts and artifact combinations associated with a sample unit should become more specialized, less varied.

Measuring changes within sites in regard to differentiation, requires more data than measuring changes in population. Such measurements usually require the excavation of whole sites. For this reason, it has been possible to predict only some general contrasts between the Basketmaker and Pueblo cultures. Nevertheless, the occurrence or nonoccurrence of these differences should provide a fair indication of whether changes in the dimension of differentiation occurred during the transition.

INTEGRATION

The dimension of integration lends itself least of all to the quantified treatment. Changes that occur in this dimension should suggest that the integration of activities is becoming more complex or effective. Since changes in this dimension were traced to changes in differentiation, evidence of a more differentiated role structure should be found. If changes in this dimension cause changes in the efficient use of technology, then the integrative changes that do occur should involve more productive processes of production or distribution.

Changes in this dimension are sought by examining three variables. First, the *kinds of groups that inhabit a particular settlement* are studied. If integration is becoming more complex, then the arrangement of family groups both within and between sites might become more complex. If such a change occurs, then it would suggest there are changes in the dimension of integration associated with the transition.

Second, changes in the differentiation of the integrative structure might occur in roles. Roles are analyzed in prehistoric populations by examining *differential treatment within burial populations.* An increase in the differentiation of integrative role structures from Basketmaker to Pueblo would indicate that a change in the dimension of integration is occurring and that this change is linked to changes in the dimension of differentiation.

Finally, *new integrative structures* might appear. The creation of ritually distinct architectural units during the transition would again indicate that changes in the dimension of integration are occurring. Thus, three variables have been suggested for which a change during the transition from Basketmaker to Pueblo would reflect underlying changes in the dimension of integration.

ENERGY

As noted in Chapter 4, good subsistence data are not available from the area where this study was carried out. However, other variables can be used. Palynological reconstructions of climate, measuring natural environmental potential, can be generated, yet to do so would represent the most naive equation of cultural and environmental change.

Similarly, changes in the quantity of storage facilities could be used in generating a crude measure of increasing community product. But, such a construction involves the assumption that all such storage space was utilized, an assumption simply not possible to make. Therefore, I omit this dimension from the test of the model. And, I intend and hope that other researchers will try to obtain sets of data that will permit the use of this dimension along with the others in the model. In the meantime, I simply note Zubrow's (1971a,b) positive test of a model, that relates carrying capacity and population and that speaks to the issues raised in this model for the case of Hay Hollow Valley.

Technology

Our ultimate concern with the growth model, is of course, determining whether we can account for the technological changes that have been used to define the Basketmaker–Pueblo transition. In this regard, our first effort will be to show that the technological changes associated with the transition do not represent random stylistic changes, but a pattern of increase in the efficiency of tool manufacture and tool use. By efficiency of tool manufacture, I mean the relative simplicity/complexity of the activities associated with tool making. By efficiency of use, I refer to the output per unit of input.

The second aspect of the effort will be demonstrating that this pattern of technological change is associated with growth as defined in the model. More specifically, we will seek answers to three questions:

1. Is the period of technological change a period of growth?
2. Is the pattern of technological change correlated with growth?
3. Are observed technological changes caused by changes in the dimensions of the growth model?

In short, my task will be to evaluate the proposed growth model by reference to predictions concerning specific linkages in that model and to evaluate the ability of the model to account for the technological changes associated with the Basketmaker–Pueblo transition.

CHAPTER EIGHT

Research Strategy

I have drawn the data used in this analysis of the Basket-maker–Pueblo transition from three sources: (1) surveys and excavations done by the Southwest Archaeological Expeditions of the Field Museum of Natural History in the summers of 1967 and 1968; (2) surveys and excavations done by the Expedition during 15 years of research in the Upper Little Colorado region; and (3) the literature of Southwestern prehistory.

Most of the data used in this analysis were drawn from the Upper Little Colorado. The ecology and culture history of this region have been thoroughly discussed by Bohrer (1968), Hevly (1964), Hill (1965), and Longacre (1963). The Upper Little Colorado was the laboratory in which the model was to be tested. How representative is this area of the Anasazi region as a whole?

The Region

The Upper Little Colorado area, as it has been studied by the Field Museum, consists of 1300 square miles lying along the southern edge of the Colorado Plateau. Local adaptation is to the Colorado

81

Plateau, rather than to the Mogollon Rim. The region was utilized prehistorically by the Folsom, Desert, Basketmaker, and Pueblo cultures. Evidence of continuous occupation appears at about A.D. 1; the area was abandoned by A.D. 1500. During this time block, the classic cultures, from Basketmaker to Regressive Pueblo, appeared.

Danson (1957:101–102) has referred to the area as a "transition zone" between the Anasazi and Mogollon traditions. When the White Mountains, the local variant of the Mogollon Rim, are included in the area, this may certainly be so. But, the attention of the Expedition has never focused on adaptations to these mountains. The central concern has been with the river valleys on the plateau itself. Ecologically, then, the sequence reflects an adaptation to the plateau.

More important, Longacre's (1963:26–40) definition of the cultural sequence in the area shows the fundamental similarity between the specific kinds of artifact and settlement-pattern changes that Kidder used in defining Basketmaker and Pueblo and those that occurred in the Upper Little Colorado. (Indeed, the changes that Kidder defined as critical probably apply to most of the Mogollon, as well as to the Anasazi, traditions. If there are differences between the two regions they lie at a far more detailed level than Kidder's definition of the essential elements of change.) Thus, ecologically and culturally, the area is appropriate for studying the Basketmaker–Pueblo transition. It is ecologically identified with the area inhabited by representatives of the Anasazi tradition and the sequence of artifactual and settlement changes is in accord with Kidder's definition. There is no reason for believing that any changes characterizing Basketmaker and Pueblo would not have been represented in the Upper Little Colorado.

Data Collection

Research done by the Museum during the summers of 1967 and 1968 provided the most critical data used in testing the hypotheses. Surveys and excavations were done in Hay Hollow Valley, east of Snowflake, Arizona. The geography and ecology of this valley and its environs have been described elsewhere (Bohrer 1968, Hevly 1964).

Hay Hollow Valley is an area of about 25 square miles within the Upper Little Colorado. There are no reasons for believing that a heavy reliance on these data might in any way affect the results.

In most instances, I will present data indicating there is general evidence from the Upper Little Colorado as a whole which supports the more detailed conclusions reached for Hay Hollow Valley. The primary difference between the valley and the region is in length of occupation. There is no Folsom adaptation in the valley, and it appears to have been abandoned 50–100 years earlier than the region.

SURVEY

The survey of the valley, which sought to collect data concerning changes in the quantity and distribution of sites, had two discrete stages. During the summer of 1967, we surveyed a block of about 5 square miles in the north end of the valley: Five square miles is an area some surveyors claim to be able to cover in a day. The decision to devote an entire summer to an area of this size was based upon the belief that many sites are missed when a region is surveyed so quickly. We desired a more detailed picture of the prehistoric utilization of the valley than results from most surveys.

Surveying was done by approximately eight people, who worked in the field 5 days a week for 10 weeks. A small area was isolated for reconnaissance by a team of three or four persons each day. They would cross and recross the area, noting all cultural occurrences. That is, the survey focused not on habitation sites alone, but on all localized clusters of nonnaturally occurring materials.

During the second season of the survey (1968), its scope was enlarged. The previous year's work at the north end of the valley provided a picture of the adaptation to the valley floor and to the top and sides of Point of the Mountain, the basalt flow forming its eastern boundary. It seemed desirable to examine the margins of the valley, as well as its center, and to consider additional possibilities of ecological variability. An area of about 20 square miles was surveyed to the east and west of the block surveyed in 1967. No attempt was made to investigate the southern margin of the area since it had been surveyed by Longacre previously and was topographically homogeneous with the area covered in 1967.

SAMPLING

To survey these 20 miles in the same detail that was applied to the original 5-mile block would have required 4 years of work. Since such a large commitment of time and personnel was unwarranted, the decision was made to sample this area. A series of experiments established that a 25% sample of the aea surveyed in 1967 would have led to the same conclusions concerning critical variables that were reached when the entire area was surveyed. The sample used was a stratified, systematic, unaligned design. The desirability of this design has been discussed by Haggett (1966).[1] The 5 square miles of territory that lay within the sample units were treated with the same care for detail exercised in 1967.

Data were recorded on a total of 325 sites. This means that in the 25 square miles investigated by the block survey and the sample, there are probably about 1000 sites. In most careful Southwestern surveys, about 50 sites are average for a 25-square-mile area. The data recovered by the survey are recorded in Appendix I.

EXCAVATION AND TESTING

In order to measure the variables related to intersite variation, a series of pithouses, again in Hay Hollow Valley, was excavated. Prior research in the Upper Little Colorado indicated that the late pithouse adaptation in the region is typified by small villages of 2–10 houses. Large villages of 20 or more houses do occur, but not at the end of the pithouse adaptation.

The 1967 survey suggested that small villages were distributed along the western side of Hay Hollow Wash, on the floor of the Valley. Our investigation centered in an area of about 75,000m² beside the wash. There were scattered areas of surface debris indicative of pithouses in several spots within the boundaries of this area. The debris also indicated that the pithouses dated to the period A.D. 600–800.

In the 75,000 m² area we expected to find clusters of a few pithouses each. Nevertheless, our investigation began with the assumption that the area contained only one village. By applying a regression equation

---

[1]At the meeting of the Society for American Archaeology at Miami Beach, Florida, in 1972, a number of papers made empirical comments on the desirability of different designs for archeologists. It is no longer clear that stratified, systematic, unaligned samples are the best. It is clear that work in progress will soon indicate which techniques are best.

I will discuss later, it was possible to determine that if this area were a single village, it should contain about 300 pithouses.

The entire area was then investigated. Each of the concentrations of cultural debris was tested to a depth at which either the presence or the absence of a pithouse was evident. The area between these concentrations was sampled using heavy machinery. Randomly distributed scrapes 3–4 feet wide and 6–12 inches deep and trenches 1 foot wide and 2–3 feet deep were dug in these interstices.

We determined that five pithouses and a similar number of intensive-activity loci were within the area. These sites occurred in three clusters near the southeast, southwest, and northwest corners of the 75,000 m² rectangle. The two clusters at the southern end of the rectangle were about 125 m apart and were separated from the clusters at the northern end by 400 m. We satisfied ourselves that we were dealing not with a single large village, but with isolated clusters of a few pithouses and activity loci. As stated previously, there is reason to believe that this pattern is a continuous one along the wash.

The hypotheses under consideration warranted a primary focus on the pithouses, with some attention to activity areas adjacent to the pithouses, as well as to the limited-activity areas. We chose a sampling design appropriate to this end: Each pithouse was excavated to its entirety; 50% of the 2-m squares in the rows adjacent to the house were excavated; 25% of the squares in the next tier of rows were excavated; and 10% in a final tier. In the localities without houses, the portion of an activity area in which features were located was excavated in its entirety. A simple random sample of the remaining squares in an area of about 800 m² surrounding the activity locus was excavated. The excavation was done in terms of four levels:

1. Surface
2. Level 1: a stratum of uncompacted sand, usually about 6 inches deep
3. Level 2: a stratum of hard silt over 1 m thick
4. Level 3: living floors within Level 2

After excavations were complete in the localities that were examined intensively, a backhoe–frontend loader was used to scrape away the unexcavated surface to determine what major features, if any, were missed. Any such features were noted. The data from the excavation, including carbon-14 dates, tree-ring dates, floral, faunal, and pollen analyses are recorded in Appendix II.

Other Sources of Data

While I drew most of the critical data in this analysis from 2 years of research, 1967–1968, data collected by the Expedition during the 13 previous years in the Upper Little Colorado region were also used. Fifteen pueblos and five pithouse villages have been excavated or tested by the Expedition, and the resulting data are detailed and usually available in quantified form. The area was surveyed by John B. Rinaldo and William A. Longacre over a 7-year period. Other areas in the Southwest have more excavated sites and a greater catalogue of survey sites, but detailed information, especially quantified information, is not available for these regions: Chaco Canyon and Mesa Verde are cases in point. The research of Paul S. Martin over the past 30 years stands alone in the comprehensiveness of reporting of excavation and survey results. For this reason, it offers an opportunity to examine variables that cannot be analyzed using data from elsewhere in the Southwest.

Finally, I have used information drawn from the literature of Southwestern prehistory in general. I have relied heavily on information from Mesa Verde and Chaco Canyon. Because these areas have been under intensive study for over 50 years, more sites have been excavated in them than in any other part of the Southwest, and the catalogue of surveyed sites is correspondingly large. For these two regions in particular, and the Southwest in general, the quality and detail of published data are less than is desirable. Nevertheless, the Southwest has probably been more intensively investigated than any other region in the world and offers almost unlimited opportunities for hypothesis-testing using already excavated sites.

CHAPTER NINE

Patterns of Demographic Change

The first variables that must be quantified in order to evaluate the model in a prehistoric context measure changes in the dimension of population: population change, sites per square mile, rooms per site, mean distance between sites, and nearest neighbor.

To suggest that archeologists can infer population change from archeological data is to suggest nothing new; such inferences have a long history in the discipline. Burial counts, site counts, room counts, the size of shell middens, and vessel capacity per living floor are used for this purpose. Because burial counts are not readily available for the Upper Little Colorado, I have used site and room counts for inferring population.

The use of site and room counts to infer population rests upon the assumption that a continuous relationship exists between the area a given group (family or community) occupies and the number of individuals in the group. That is to say, the more persons there are in a group, the larger the space the group occupies. If this assumption is correct, then one can estimate the number of individuals inhabiting a given settlement or house or region by knowing the room area being utilized.

The assumption that there is a relationship between area and population has been subjected to some empirical scrutiny. Two geographers, Stewart and Warntz (1967), have examined the relationship between community size and population for 157 English and Welsh cities. Their analysis shows that as the area of a community increases, its population increases. Cook and Heizer (1965) and Narroll (1962) have tested this assumption on ethnographic data; their conclusions also support its viability.

Hill (1965: 202–211) examined the relationship between area and population for the particular case of the ethnographic Southwest in reconstructing the population of Broken K Pueblo. Hayes (1964) and Eddy (1966) employed similar techniques in arriving at population estimates for Wetherill Mesa and the Navajo Reservoir district respectively. Turner and Lofgren (1966) have used vessel capacity to estimate population and have shown that this measure corresponds to Colton's (1960) estimate based on room counts.

The technique used here is based on the assumption discussed above and infers population from changes in the number of habitation rooms. I feel such a measure is more accurate than one based on the total number of sites or the total number of rooms. If all sites are included, changes in the number of limited-activity sites or nonhabitation sites influence the inference. If all rooms are included, changes in storage space that are independent of changes in habitation space affect the inference. A measure based upon habitation rooms hews more strictly to the assumption underlying the inference being made.

Habitation Room Counts

The procedure I used to arrive at the habitation room counts consisted of six steps:

1. Location of sites with habitation rooms
2. Estimation of the number of rooms on the site
3. Estimation of the number of habitation rooms on the site
4. Dating of the site
5. Correction for the developmental history of the site
6. Summation of the data

I applied this procedure to four regions in the Hay Hollow Valley—a survey block labeled "South," investigated by Longacre in the early

1960s, a block labeled "North," investigated by the Expedition in the summer of 1967, and two blocks labeled "East" and "West," sampled in the summer of 1968—as follows.

1. Location of sites: The sites were located using the survey techniques described earlier.

2. Estimation of the number of rooms on the site: The number of rooms on a site that has been surveyed, but not excavated, can be estimated. Most, if not all, archeologists make such estimates, basing their conclusion on the recognition that the size of the rubble mound or artifact scatter provides an indication of the number of rooms on the site. In some instances the room count is arrived at by an apparently subjective measure. Sounder procedure warrants the measurement of some dimension of the mound. Hayes (1964) in the Wetherill Mesa survey used measurements of the length of sites to arrive at a room estimate.

In this research, I used a relationship between the area of a site and the number of rooms on it. The following equations describe this relationship:

Pithouses: Number of pithouses = .0047 site area in square meters + 1.2.

Pueblos: Number of rooms + .10 site area in square meters + 4.0.

Site area in the case of pithouses is the extent of the refuse scatter. In the case of pueblos, it is the size of the rubble mound. The equations are both significant at the .01 level.

I derived these equations by regression analysis from measurement of already excavated sites. For pueblos, the sample consisted of 10 sites excavated by the Southwest Expedition over the past 15 years of work in western New Mexico and eastern Arizona. I fitted the relationship between the area of the rubble mound prior to excavation and the number of rooms uncovered to the least-squares equation presented above.

An insufficient number of pithouses for achieving a statistically significant generalization were excavated in the immediate area. Therefore, I expanded the sample to 10 pithouse sites by including sites from the Pine Lawn Valley, the Forestdale Valley, and the Point of Pines region. Again, a least-squares solution was found, in this instance to the relationship between artifact scatter and number of houses within the scatter.

In surveying, the size of rubble mounds or refuse scatter was measured, the appropriate equation applied to the measurement, and

the number of rooms on the site estimated. Where surface indications
were clear, the equation estimate was checked against a count of the
number of pueblo rooms or pithouses; there was a close correspondence between the two. For each site with architecture, we
made an estimate of the total number of rooms on the site.

   3.   Estimation of the number of habitation rooms on the site: Not
all the rooms on a pueblo site are habitation rooms. Sites have ceremonial and storage rooms. If the number of such rooms remained constant through time, there would be no difficulty; however, constancy
is not the case. Pithouse villages are composed almost entirely of
habitation rooms. The ratio of storage rooms to habitation rooms
is greater in late pueblos than in earlier ones (Hill 1965: 246). I
felt this information should be taken into account, that room estimates
should be adjusted so as to include only habitation rooms. The procedure employed was: (1) Count all pithouses on pithouse sites; (2) subtract 25% of the total number of rooms from pueblo villages occupied
A.D. 900–1150; (3) subtract 41% of the total number of rooms
from pueblos occupied A.D. 1150–1500. This operation provided an
estimate, not of the total number of rooms per site, but of the number of nonstorage rooms per site.

   4.   Dating of the site: Paul S. Martin (Breternitz 1966) dated sites
on the basis of tree-ring-dated pottery types, assigning each site to
one or more 50-year time intervals. Assigning the site to more than
one such interval takes into account two variables. First, many sites,
especially large ones, are in fact occupied for periods of 200 or more
years. An independent check on this statement is the use of carbon-14
or tree rings to date the site without the intermediate use of pottery.
Second, there is some error in all dating techniques. Assigning a
site to a span of, say, 250 years indicates that the site was more likely
to have been inhabited in the middle of the span, with decreasing
probability of habitation at either end of the span.

   5.   Correction for the developmental history of the site: Pueblo
sites are not built in a day. Therefore, given a time span during
which a particular site was occupied, it is necessary to make assumptions about the architectural history of the site—the rates at which
rooms were built and abandoned. Recent research provides increasingly sure grounds for formulating such assumptions.

   Dean (1967) has performed a room-by-room analysis of tree-ring
samples for Betatakin and Kiet Siel pueblos. His research suggested
that pueblos are not erected in a short period of time, but grow

by the cumulative addition of room blocks. Furthermore, some rooms are being abandoned while others are in the process of being constructed. A study by Hill (1965: 203) indicated that the maximum number of rooms actually occupied at one time on a site is about 78% of the total number of rooms on the site.

To take these factors into account, I constructed growth curves for individual sites with the following characteristics. (1) Maximum occupation of the site is assumed to occur at the midpoint of the span of occupation. (2) Maximum occupancy is 78% of the total habitation rooms on the site. (3) Each period moving away from the midpoint in either direction is assumed to have an occupation of half the rooms used during the preceding period.

Thus, a site with 100 habitation rooms occupied for 200 years (four 50-year periods) is recorded as follows:

$$39/78/78/39$$

This technique also takes into account the problem of precisely dating the site. When a time span is assigned to a site, the probability that the site was occupied is greater at the midpoint than at either end of the span. In this sense, the midpoint of the span receives a greater weight than do periods near the ends of the distribution.

6. Summation of the data: The final step is the summation of individual site curves in order to arrive at a curve for the region under study.

This technique of reconstructing population has been criticized for its large number of underlying assumptions. While the criticism is in one sense true, it implies that there is another way of treating data which does not involve assumptions. Every technique of reconstruction involves assumptions. The question that must be asked is whether the assumptions are good or poor ones.

I suspect that the critics of this technique prefer the standard practice of counting the number of sites or rooms per phase. This procedure does indeed involve assumptions, and not very good ones. Almost any archeologist, in using artifacts or isotopes to date the occupation of a site, can specify a point or limited span that he believes represents the most probable occupation of the site. He can also represent increasingly longer spans when he thinks the probability of occupation is smaller. Such knowledge should be taken into account; for when the time span of occupation is represented as a phase, the investigator is arguing that the probability of occupation is equal throughout the phase.

Similarly, we know that sites do not come into existence in one year and go out of existence as fast—sites only gradually increase and decrease in size. Yet, this assumption is made in counting all rooms on a site for an entire phase.

All archeologists are aware of the imprecision of their data. But imprecision is no antidote to imprecision. When sites are counted for an entire phase, there is a comfortable feeling that by using large categories, the imprecision is reduced. Using imprecise categories does not create precision. Even the crudest probability function representing site occupancy will provide a more acceptable characterization of population at a site than assuming homogeneity through time.

It is for these reasons that I have used the assumptions set forth here.

Population in Hay Hollow Valley

I used the techniques discussed above in plotting curves for the four survey blocks in Hay Hollow Valley. The results of these analyses appear in Table 9.1. Before considering the conclusions to be drawn from these curves, several problems should be discussed.

First, it is important to know whether this curve is unique to the valley or whether it can be generated for the Upper Little Colorado region. It might be, for example, that Hay Hollow Valley is a part of a population system encompassing other localities. In this case, the peaks and dips in the curves would represent the ebb and flow of population between the two regions. To check for this possibility, I employed Longacre's (1963) survey data for the region. The site map for the Upper Little Colorado shows that sites are not equally distributed, but occur in a series of local clusters. I have named these clusters for their geographical locality: St. Johns, Lyman Reservoir, Hooper Ranch, Water Canyon, Vernon, and Mesa Redonda. In each of these areas, Longacre discovered 15–65 sites. Each is a relatively dense cluster of sites separated by 4–10 miles from another dense cluster.

If the Upper Little Colorado region were characterized by multilocality population systems, then there should be pairs of localities such that as one locality in each pair undergoes a rise in population, the

TABLE 9.1
Dwelling Units in Hay Hollow Valley: By Blocks and Total

Time period (A.D.)	North block	South block	East block	West block	Total
200–250	2	0	0	4	6
250–300	3	0	0	8	11
300–350	13	0	0	15	28
350–400	26	0	0	28	54
400–450	51	0	0	64	115
450–500	51	0	0	64	115
500–550	44	1	0	28	73
550–600	46	4	0	15	65
600–650	42	15	0	8	65
650–700	31	23	6	4	64
700–750	17	32	17	0	66
750–800	14	30	20	0	64
800–850	13	43	28	5	89
850–900	20	55	25	9	109
900–950	22	67	15	12	116
950–1000	54	66	8	18	146
1000–1050	61	44	24	27	156
1050–1100	63	22	37	25	147
1100–1150	59	41	20	14	134
1150–1200	56	81	20	17	174
1200–1250	52	81	26	7	166
1250–1300	27	41	26	0	94
1300–1350	0	0	15	0	15
1350–1400	0	0	5	0	5
1400–1450	0	0	2	0	2

other falls, and vice versa. Using the same techniques as for Hay Hollow Valley, population curves were plotted for each other locality. Without exception, these curves duplicated the curve discovered for the valley. The only difference in the curves was the occupation of sites along the Upper Little Colorado River for a 100–150-year period after the valley was abandoned. Otherwise, there is no reason to believe the Hay Hollow Valley curve does not accurately typify the population changes for the Upper Little Colorado region.

Second, I do not believe there is any point in using a curve such as this one to arrive at exact estimates of the population of the area. That is, I see no point in making statements of the type: At A.D. 700, 1500 persons lived in the valley, and by A.D. 1000, population had increased to 2000. The value of curves such as this one is in their shape, not their level. If the occupancy-per-habitation-unit ratio remains constant over time, then changes in habitation rooms reflect changes in population, regardless of what the exact population was.

Is there a sound basis for concluding that the number of persons in a habitation room remains relatively constant over time? Hill (1965: 205) employing data from Steward (1937), Parsons (1929), Kroeber (1917), Donaldson (1893), Beaglehole (1935), and Titiev (1944), arrived at an estimate of 6.1 persons per room at Broken K Pueblo. Turner and Lofgren (1966), using partially the same and partially different data, found an average of 5.3. If a problem exists with respect to the number of persons per habitation room, it lies in the difference between these estimates for pueblo populations and a similar one for pithouses. Did the pithouse population per habitation room match that of the pueblo?

Two lines of evidence may be brought to bear on this problem. First, when a series of excavated pithouses from the valley are examined and their areas compared to those of pueblo units, the results are similar. Slightly fewer than six persons probably inhabited the average pithouse. In other words, the area of a pithouse is about the same as that of a pueblo habitation-storage room unit.

A second line of reasoning revolves around the Navajo, who live in structures with design and function similar to that of the pithouse. These structures approximate the size of a pithouse, being, on the average, somewhat larger. Kluckholn and Leighton (1962: 90, 103) indicate that hogans are about 7.5 m in diameter on the average and hold an average of 7.35 persons. Johnston's (1966: 45) more detailed demographic study found an average of 3.93–5.00 persons per hogan. Turner and Lofgren (1966: 129) estimate that 4.5–4.8 persons was average for Southwestern adaptation prior to A.D. 900, and 5.1–5.2 for adaptations after this date. Such a slight discrepancy would scarcely affect the shape of the curve. If anything, it would mean that the difference between the Basketmaker and Pueblo population maximums was greater than Table 9.1 indicates.

The following observations are supported by Table 9.1.

1. A.D. 200–400: Population increased.
2. The peak of the population for the Basketmaker culture was reached at about A.D. 400.
3. A.D. 500–800: Population decreased and became stable.
4. A.D. 800–1050: Population increased rapidly.
5. Population reached and remained at a maximum for Pueblo

culture A.D. 1050–1200. This maximum was 50–100% larger than that attained by Basketmaker culture.

6. After A.D. 1200, the population declined rapidly. The valley was abandoned by about A.D. 1350, although the Upper Little Colorado region was occupied for another 150 years.

A knowledge of population alone would be insufficient for understanding the prehistory of this region in terms of the model proposed. I underscored the importance of viewing the locus of population. Therefore, from the data I have derived three measures of the density of population in the area: sites per square mile, mean distance between sites, and nearest neighbor. The measurement of the first two is straightforward, and the results are shown in Table 9.2.

The interpretation of the nearest neighbor statistic, also in Table 9.2, is somewhat more complex. This statistic is based upon a comparison of the actual spatial distribution of a number of units and the distribution that ought to occur under conditions of random variation. This is measured on a scale on which a figure of 0 would be obtained for a situation in which the sites were completely aggregated, actually adjacent to each other; a figure of 1 is attained under conditions of random distribution; and a figure of 2.15 is obtained when the units are equally spaced.

With this new information, more complex statements concerning the demographic changes in Hay Hollow Valley are possible.

1. Population increased from A.D. 200 until A.D. 400. This increase was associated with a relatively constant number of sites per square mile and a very even spacing of sites. Thus, the increase was accounted for by the internal growth of relatively few sites. This fact is reflected in an increasing average number of rooms per site.
2. A.D. 500–800: Population decreased. Sites were seven times more dense and were randomly spaced. The decline in a few large sites was offset to some extent by an increase in the number of small ones.
3. Population increased rapidly A.D. 800–1050. The number of sites per square mile also increased rapidly, and sites were more closely spaced than during the previous period. The number of rooms per site remained relatively constant.
4. A.D. 1050–1200: Population was at a maximum. Density began to decrease, and sites were randomly distributed. The average

TABLE 9.2
Density in Hay Hollow Valley

Time period (A.D.)	Sites per square mile[a]	Rooms per site	Mean distance between sites[b]	Nearest neighbor[b]
200–250	0.15	2	—	—
250–300	0.20	3	.78	.71
300–350	0.20	7	.95	.88
350–400	0.20	13	.95	.88
400–450	0.25	23	.95	.88
450–500	0.25	23	.95	.88
500–550	0.55	7	.39	.70
550–600	0.60	5	.39	.70
600–650	0.95	3	.25	.55
650–700	1.00	3	.23	.44
700–750	1.05	3	.41	.73
750–800	1.00	3	.41	.73
800–850	1.15	4	.78	.89
850–900	1.30	4	.30	.52
900–950	1.65	4	.33	.72
950–1000	3.00	2	.19	.73
1000–1050	3.10	2	.21	.78
1050–1100	2.70	3	.23	.78
1100–1150	2.20	3	.19	.68
1150–1200	0.75	12	.54	.78
1200–1250	0.55	15	.82	.99
1250–1300	0.45	10	.73	.99
1300–1350	0.15	5	—	—
1350–1400	0.10	3	—	—
1400–1450	0.05	2	—	—

[a]Based on an estimated 20 square miles.
[b]North survey block only.

number of rooms per site began to increase at the end of the period.

5. A.D. 1200 to the abandonment of the region (A.D. 1300), population and density decreased. The aggregation of sites decreased, and the number of rooms per site increased, and then declined. Large sites, then, were associated with a general population decrease and were probably associated with less than ideal conditions (Hill 1965).

If one focuses on three periods—Basketmaker, Pueblo, and a transition period—rather than on the specific changes in the population curves, a definite pattern is evident. The pithouse adaptation in the valley is characterized by a few large, relatively well-spaced cites. Demographic changes are accounted for primarily by changes in the size of these few sites. For the transitional period, sites are small, density is high, and spacing varies from aggregated to random. This suggests a drastic reorganization from the pithouse adaptation.

At the population peak of the Pueblo adaptation, sites are still relatively small, but they are dense and randomly spaced. The large sites associated with Classic Pueblo occur not at the peak of population associated with the Pueblo adaptation to Hay Hollow Valley, but with the decline.

Summary

Did these data support the conclusion that there were significant changes in the dimension of population during the transition period? The proposition that significant changes in this dimension occurred was to be accepted if, for A.D. 700–1000:

1. The rate of population increase was at a maximum, and the result of the population increase was a maximum of population for the valley.
2. The rate of increase in the number of sites per square mile was at a maximum and resulted in an absolute maximum for the valley.
3. The rate of increase in dwelling units per site was at a maximum and resulted in an absolute maximum for the valley.
4. The nearest neighbor statistic shows that the transition was associated with a maximum aggregation of sites.

A.D. 800–1050, population increased by 100 dwelling units, or 20 dwelling units per 50-year period. The only comparable increase occurred A.D. 200–450, when 107 dwelling units, or 21 dwelling units per 50-year period, were added. Because of the difficulties in recognizing and securely dating prepottery sites, it was impossible to be certain about the magnitude of this initial increase.

At A.D. 700, there were 1.05 sites per square mile in the valley. Between A.D. 1000 and 1050, there were 2.70. The number of sites per square mile tripled during the transition period. The only other period of rapid increase was at the beginning of the sequence and was subject to the same indefiniteness as the population figures.

Site-spacing underwent significant changes during the transition. Mean distance between sites A.D. 500–1150 was at one-half the value outside these dates. The periods A.D. 600–700 and A.D. 950–1150 were associated with even closer spacing. The nearest neighbor results were not clear cut, although in general, they suggested a random settlement pattern throughout most of the sequence: A.D. 600–700 and A.D. 850–900, the statistic was somewhat lower.

Thus, in the variables chosen to evaluate the probability that significant changes in the dimension of population occurred during the transition, except in dwelling units per site and nearest neighbor, the predictions were accurate. While the fit to the period A.D. 700–1000 was by no means perfect, the predicted changes fell predominantly within this period for each variable. Change in the dimension of population was associated with the transition. A change in density that could account for change in the dimension of differentiation occurred at the regional, but not at the per site, level.

Generalizing the Case

Population is the one dimension for which generalizations can be made concerning most of the Southwest. The period A.D. 500–1000 encompassed the transition for most of the Southwest. Rapid population increases during this period are known from the Flagstaff region (Colton 1960; Turner and Lofgren 1966), the Cohonina area (Schwartz 1956), the Hopi mesas (Hack 1942), Mesa Verde (Hayes 1964), and the Navajo Reservoir district (Eddy 1966). Population increase during the transition period seems to have been a widespread phenomenon.

CHAPTER TEN

The Changing Organization of Work

Archeologists study variables that measure the dimension of differentiation. Gabel (1967) discusses a number of different approaches to this dimension, which include topics such as the division of labor, craft specialists, and productive processes. The basic insight upon which such studies are based is no more complex than the recognition that the tools and facilities associated with a steel mill are different from those associated with a drugstore or a home.

Facilities are a first basis for making inferences concerning differentiation. In some cultures, a whole set of indoor activities are performed under a single roof. Other cultures break this same set of activities into a number of components, each performed in a room of its own, with appropriate structural modifications. In still a third culture, the activities may no longer be associated with one set of rooms. Instead, craft specialism, in which functionally similar rooms occur together, may be practiced.

Similarly, tools are a set of data from which differentiation can be inferred. A room that is the locus of generalized activities will contain a diffuse tool kit. A room that is the locus of specialized activities will contain functionally interrelated tools. Hill (1965) and

99

Reals (1965) have used differential distributions of tools in studying the utilization of activity space within sites.

Variation in the distribution of tools has also been used in inferring intersite differentiation of function (Binford and Binford 1965; Gardin 1965a). The principle is the same as that used in inferring relationships within sites. A site that is the locus of only lithic artifacts was utilized differently from one that is the locus of only pottery. Variation among the kinds of tools found on a series of sites provides a basis for inferring variation in the kinds of activities that were performed on them.

In presenting test implications for the model of change, two kinds of predictions concerning changes that ought to occur in the dimension of differentiation were made. First, intersite differentiation of activities should increase rapidly and reach a maximum during the transition period. Second, intrasite differentiation should vary in the same manner.

Intersite Variation

I sought to examine the differentiation of intersite activities in two ways; both involved limited-activity sites. Limited-activity loci are sites on which the total range of activities performed is less than that range associated with a habitation site. I am assuming that habitation sites are the locus of the most complete set of the aggregate of activities carried out by an adaptation. On a limited-activity site, only a few of these activities are performed. Recognizing differences between the two site types in field situations is possible, but more difficult than this neat verbal distinction implies.

During the 1967 field season, 181 limited-activity sites were catalogued. In the summer of 1968, 60 more sites were found. Thirteen different types of limited activity sites were defined. Ten of these were used in the analysis and 3 were not.

The first type of limited-activity site that was *not* used in the analysis is a petroglyph site. These sites are drawings pecked into the surface of naturally occurring boulders. Since they are not datable, they provide information that is not usable in the analysis. Nine such sites were located in the survey.

The second type of activity site that was *not* used consists of sites for which some critical bits of data, either the size of the site or its date, were unobtainable. Thirty-five of these sites (Type X in Appendix I) were recorded.

The most important category of unanalyzed activity loci was sites

(Type 0 in Appendix I, "Hay Hollow Valley Sites") on which the only cultural debris was chipped stone tools. These sites are usually called "prepottery" sites. The name suggests that they were used prior to the invention of pottery.

I do not believe this nomenclature is justifiable. It assumes that any site on which pottery does not occur must have been used prior to the invention of pottery. Some of the prepottery sites were probably nonpottery sites. They were utilized after the invention of pottery, but pottery was not used in an activity carried on there. In the absence of funds to isotopically date such sites or to study tool typology on a level that would permit a crude seriation of the sites, it is impossible to determine whether they are in fact prepottery sites or are simply nonpottery sites. Therefore, I have not used these sites in the analysis; 46 of them have been catalogued.

Excluding these 3 types of limited-activity sites, 10 remain. They were defined on the basis of the 1967 survey data, and their efficacy was confirmed by the 1968 data. Attributes used in defining the types were: presence versus absence of pottery, presence versus absence of lithics, presence versus absence of features, and size of site.

Once the sites were grouped into types on the basis of these four attributes, the matrix was analyzed to determine if there were significant differences in the location of these sites on topographical features, and if they were differentially distributed in time. Six topographical situations were distinguished: (1) top of Point of the Mountain; (2) side of Point of the Mountain; (3) alluvial fans at base of Point of the Mountain; (4) sandstone terrace tops; (5) lower sandstone terraces; and (6) alluvial flats, hills, and knolls. While these are topographical categories, ecological studies by Hevly (1964: 22–33) have shown that to the extent soil differences are present, they also represent different plant communities. While the variable is defined as topography, it is loosely interpretable as plant community, also.

A percentage-point differential analysis indicated that 50% of the sites would have to have different topographical locations in order to conclude that there is no relation between the site types and topography. Some 32% of the sites would have to have been occupied during different time spans in order to conclude that the types do not change in frequency of occurrence over time. This analysis suggested that some of the types might occur in distinctive temporal or topographical situations.

While an insufficient number of cases was available to test this association at the most detailed level, it was possible to make meaningful distinctions between sites located on Point of the Mountain and sites located away from it, on terraces and in flatter areas, and between sites that were utilized prior to and after A.D. 850. The resulting typology is based on the original four attributes. But, where a topographical or temporal pattern is apparent, this information is built into the typology. The 10 types of limited-activity sites are as follows:

Type 1	Pottery:	Presence
	Lithics:	Presence
	Features:	Absence
	Size:	1–7 m²
	Location:	Point of the Moutain (100%)
	Date:	78% after A.D. 850
	N = 9 (1967), 4 (1968) = 13

Type 2	Pottery:	Presence
	Lithics:	Presence
	Features:	Absence
	Size:	15–75 m²
	Topography:	Prior to A.D. 850, 75% away from Point of the Mountain
		After A.D. 850, 70% on Point of the Mountain
	Date:	74% before A.D. 850
	N = 27 (1967), 8 (1968) = 35

Type 3	Pottery:	Presence
	Lithics:	Presence
	Features:	Absence
	Size:	100–1000 m²
	Topography:	Away from Point of the Mountain (91%)
	Date:	62% before A.D. 850
	N = 21 (1967), 9 (1968) = 30

Type 4	Pottery:	Presence
	Lithics:	Absence
	Features:	Absence
	Size:	1–4 m²
	Topography:	On Point of the Mountain (100%)
	Date:	83% after A.D. 850
	N = 12 (1967), 1 (1968) = 13

Type 5	Pottery:	Presence
	Lithics:	Absence
	Features:	Absence
	Size:	35–90 m²
	Topography:	Prior to A.D. 850, 100% away from Point of the Mountain
		After A.D. 850, 100% on Point of the Mountain

| Type 6 | Pottery: | Presence |
| | Lithics: | Absence |

	Features:	Presence
	Size:	2–180 m²
	Topography:	Early, 100% away from Point of the Mountain
		After A.D. 850, 75% on Point of the Mountain
	Date:	No definable pattern
	N = 4 (1967)	
Type 7	Pottery:	Presence
	Lithics:	Presence
	Features:	Presence
	Size:	1–445 m²
	Topography:	Prior to A.D. 850, away from Point of the
		Mountain (84%)
		After A.D. 850, 80% on Point of the Mountain
	Date:	No definable pattern
	N = 17 (1967), 8 (1968) = 25	
Type 8	Pottery:	Presence
	Lithics:	Presence
	Features:	Presence
	Size:	900+ m²
	Topography:	Prior to A.D. 850, away from Point of the
		Mountain (67%)
		After A.D. 850, on Point of the Mountain (100%)
	Date:	No definable pattern
	N = 6 (1967), 2 (1968) = 8	
Type 9	Pottery:	Presence
	Lithics:	Presence (in naturally occurring sources of flint)
	Features:	Absence
	Size:	63–100 m²
	Topography:	Away from Point of the Mountain (100%)
	Date:	Prior to A.D. 850 (75%)
	N = 4 (1967)	
Type 10	Pottery:	Presence
	Lithics:	Presence (with quantities of basalt cobbles)
	Features:	Absence
	Size:	10–400 m²
	Topography:	Away from Point of the Mountain (95%)
	Date:	Prior to A.D. 850 (82%)
	N = 11 (1967), 6 (1968) = 17[1]	

[1]These data suggest an interesting pattern pertinent to the strategic model of change. Before A.D. 850, when sites tended to be located on Point of the Mountain, limited activity sites occurred away from it. As habitation was increasingly confined to the valley floor, more limited activity sites were found on Point of the Mountain. Both are a part of an adaptations site location strategy. But, one would assume that limited activity loci are the more marginal. Thus, loci that had been marginal prior to A.D. 850 became central after that date.

After the different types of limited-activity sites were defined, data from the North Survey Block were used in two ways. First, the total amount of space utilized as limited-activity sites at a series of points in time was compared with total area used for habitation. The results of this analysis, which are summarized in Table 10.1, indicate a consistent pattern.

1. A.D. 400–700: For each 1 m of activity space on a limited-activity site, there were 10 m² on a habitation site.
2. A.D. 700–800: The ratio was about 1 : 2.
3. A.D. 800–900: There was 1 m² activity space on a limited-activity site for each 1 m² on a habitation site.
4. A.D. 900–1200: The ratio returns to 1 : 2.
5. After A.D. 1200, the ratio becomes 1 : 8.

TABLE 10.1
Comparison of Areas of Limited-Activity Sites
and Habitation Sites in North Survey Block

Time period (A.D.)	Total area of habitation sites (m²)	Total area of limited-activity sites (m²)
400–500	2,900	300
500–600	16,000	2,100
600–700	15,000	1,900
700–800	6,000	3,400
800–900	10,500	10,600
900–1000	18,500	9,100
1000–1100	15,900	9,200
1100–1200	13,600	8,800
1200–1300	2,300	300

In short, limited-activity sites accounted for as much culturally utilized space as habitation sites for the period A.D. 300–900. For A.D. 700–800 and A.D. 900–1200, one-third of the culturally manipulated space was accounted for by these sites. These data seem to indicate that the differentiation of activities was at a maximum A.D. 700–1200. To the extent that the space used for activities is an indication of where the activities were performed, the activities were most fragmented during this period.

In order to test the validity of this conclusion, a more detailed analysis was performed. Diversity in the kinds of limited-activity sites that were present at different points in time and diversity in the topographical situations that were being utilized were analyzed. The coefficient of variability was used, and the results of the analysis occur in Table 10.2.

The coefficient of variability has a range 0–1. A statistic of 1 indicates that a given distribution is homogenous; one or two classificatory categories account for most of the cases. A statistic of 0 indicates that a given distribution is heterogenous: The cases tend to be evenly distributed over a number of categories.

Table 10.2 is interpreted as follows. For the period A.D. 900–1200, the different types of limited-activity sites were well represented; no one type tended to account for the majority of the cases. Prior to, and after A.D. 1200, this was no longer true. For the periods A.D. 200–900 and A.D. 1200–1400, a few types of sites tended to account for most of the cases. Diversity measured as the presence of many types of sites was at a maximum A.D. 900–1000.

The same conclusion is reached when diversity in the use of topographical situations is considered. The coefficients for A.D. 900–1200 were lower than those before and after this period. During this period, different topographical situations were utilized relatively equally. Before and after this period, only a few of the topographical categories were used. Using this test, diversity in intersite activity sites was again found to be at a maximum A.D. 900–1000.

TABLE 10.2
Diversity in the Presence of Types of Limited-Activity Sites and in the Use of Topographical Situations in North Survey Block

Time period (A.D.)	Coefficient of variability for site types	Coefficient of variability for topography
400–500	.77	.74
500–600	.68	.73
600–700	.77	.76
700–800	.60	.72
800–900	.57	.82
900–1000	.35	.48
1000–1100	.42	.54
1100–1200	.42	.54
1200+	.78	.76

Differentiation within Sites

Processes of differentiation of activity loci also operate within sites. An analysis of both artifacts and architecture suggested that increasingly specific activity areas appeared within sites. Prior to A.D. 1, two types of activity space were evident, indoor and outdoor. Most variability seemed to follow this distinction fairly strictly. At around A.D. 600–700, a second form of indoor space appeared. Habitation rooms existed, but there were also proto-kivas, rooms with the architectural attributes of kivas, but containing artifacts suggesting specialized male activities. By A.D. 1000, there were three kinds of indoor space, habitation space, storage space, and kiva or ceremonial space.

The data upon which these generalizations were based were drawn from three sites excavated by the Expedition 1964–1969. The County Road site was excavated by the Expedition in 1964 and was occupied prior to A.D. 1. The Gurley sites, dating to around A.D. 700, were excavated during the summer of 1968. Broken K Pueblo, which dates to around A.D. 1100, was excavated during the summers of 1962 and 1963.

Reals's (1965) analysis of the artifacts from the County Road site indicated the existence of two discrete kinds of activity space, indoor and outdoor. She believed that indoor space was utilized predominantly by females and outdoor space by males. Using factor analysis, she broke the indoor space into two discrete components and suggested that it was used for cooking and for grinding. Outdoor space was used for butchering, hide preparation, toolmaking, and, in one restricted area, roasting.

The distribution of these activities was somewhat less than perfectly discrete. Only 20 of the excavated 2-m squares (26%) were clearly associated with a single activity. In another 26% of the squares, it was impossible to define one activity as predominant. In the remaining 48%, a single factor accounted for most of the variability. In most of the squares, at least three factors were represented, and the dominant factor accounted for little more than 50% of the variability.

By the time that Broken K Pueblo was inhabited, the situation was considerably changed. On the basis of artifact and pollen analysis, Hill (1965: 147–148) defined three different kinds of roofed space. Habitation rooms were the most general purpose kind of room. Hill demonstrated that food preparation, eating, water storage and use, tool manufacture, and pottery manufacture occurred in these rooms. The rooms were specialized in the sense that they were the one kind of room in which a variety of different activities was carried out.

Storage rooms were used predominantly for storage. Hill believed that other activities may have occasionally overflowed into these rooms. But, their primary use was as storage space.

The final type of roofed space at Broken K was the kiva (Hill 1965: 148). These rooms were used for ceremonial activities, for weaving, and for tool manufacturing.

Outdoor space was used in a fashion similar to its use at the County Road site. Roasting, in particular, and scraping and tool manufacture occurred here.

Hill ended his discussion by stressing the multifunctionality of space utilization at Broken K. In comparison to the manner in which we use space today, most of the space at Broken K was multifunctional, but in comparison to the manner in which it was used at the County Road site, the space at Broken K had become increasingly functionally specific. The similarities between habitation rooms and outdoor space at Broken K, and pithouses and outdoor space at the County Road site was evident. But there were no houses at County Road, which in terms of either facilities or artifacts, could be called kivas or storage rooms. Even within the sphere of habitation rooms, there was evidence of greater specialization at Broken K than at the County Road site.

McCutcheon (1968) used the coefficient of variation to show that habitation rooms at Broken K tended to be more discretely associated with one of Reals's activity factors than were the houses at the County Road site. Three of the five factors showed greater room-to-room variability at Broken K Pueblo than at the County Road site. The average factor variability of .51 at the County Road site was exceeded by a .69 average at Broken K. These statistics simply demonstrated a tendency for a room at Broken K to be more discretely associated with a single factor than a room at County Road.

An important bit of evidence of specialization that did not exist at County Road was the evidence of specialization in production at Broken K. Pendants, bone rings, and similar artifacts were distributed throughout the village. But the graving tools that would have been utilized in making such artifacts were localized in the northwestern corner of the Pueblo (Longacre 1966: 100). Antler flakes, wrenches, saws, and blades were also localized in this part of the pueblo. Arrowshaft tools, on the other hand, were localized in its southern portion (Longacre 1966: 100). Longacre (1966) interpreted these data as follows: "I suggest that a pattern of reciprocal exchange of products (and probably services as well) was operative at this prehistoric pueblo [p. 100]." There were no data from the County Road site that even remotely suggests specialization in the production of artifacts.

In order to discover when changes in the interim between these two sites occurred, the Expedition undertook the excavation of four pithouses and their associated activity areas. (The techniques used in discovering and excavating the Gurley sites are discussed in Chapter 8.) Although the pattern is not clear cut, carbon-14 and tree-ring dates suggested that the houses were occupied at about A.D. 700. (Dating is discussed more thoroughly in Appendix II.) Pithouses 1 and 2 were most certainly contemporaneous and may have been occupied somewhat before A.D. 700. Pithouse X may be somewhat later, and Pithouse Y still later. Pithouses 1 and 2 were about 3 m from each other. Pithouses X and Y were a few hundred meters from each other and from the other two pithouses.

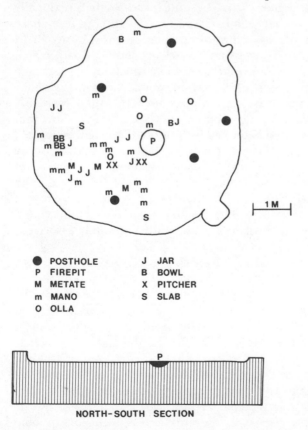

●	POSTHOLE	J	JAR
P	FIREPIT	B	BOWL
M	METATE	X	PITCHER
m	MANO	S	SLAB
O	OLLA		

NORTH-SOUTH SECTION

Figure 10.1. The Gurley sites: Pithouse 1.

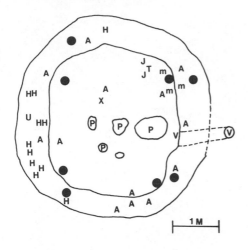

POSTHOLE
P FIREPIT
H HAMMERSTONE
A SLAB
m MANO
J JAR

B BOWL
T PALETTE
X MORTAR
V VENTILATOR
U SPINDLEWHORL

Figure 10.2. The Gurley sites: Pithouse X.

Three different kinds of space can be defined using the data from the Gurley sites. A first kind of space was represented by Pithouses 1 and Y (see Figures 10.1 and 10.4). Pithouse 1 contained a far more complete artifact assemblage. On the living surface were found 3 intact metates, 15 manos, and 10–15 pottery vessels. While fewer artifacts were present, House Y followed this same pattern. Pithouse 1 had a hearth, and Pithouse Y probably did also. Thus, these two houses follow the pattern of habitation rooms in the County Road site and Broken K Pueblo.

Pithouse X and Pithouse 2 represent very different patterns (see Figures 10.2 and 10.3). Architecturally, these two houses are kivas. They had ventilators (that of Pithouse 2 was removed by the backhoe), benches, and roof entrances. In terms of artifacts, they do not fall completely within the realm of kivas. The assemblage of Pithouse X was more complete than that in Pithouse 2. Pecked slabs and hammerstones were the predominant artifact types in this house. A spindle whorl lay on the bench. A cloudblower was in the fill against the bench and may have fallen from it. One-half of a metate was found on the floor. It had been pecked in much the same manner as the

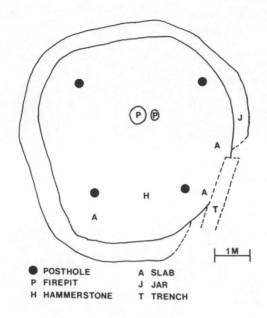

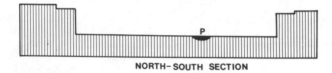

NORTH-SOUTH SECTION

Figure 10.3. The Gurley sites: Pithouse 2.

slabs, suggesting that it was not used as a metate. The manos present could have been used with either the mortar or palette, which were on the floor.

The differences between these two types of pithouses become evident in comparing maps of artifact distributions on their floors. Pithouses X and 2 were the locus of very specialized activities. The presence of hammerstones as well as a number of cores, utilized flakes, and small firepits, suggests that toolmaking was a primary activity. The spindle whorl indicates that weaving may also have occurred in such rooms. Since the cloudblower was not on the floor, there was no clear evidence of ritual. Some juniper-seed beads and parts of a bone bracelet or necklace were found on the floor.

None of the houses at the Gurley sites seems to have had a storage function. The pottery vessels in Pithouse 1, even if pitchers, bowls,

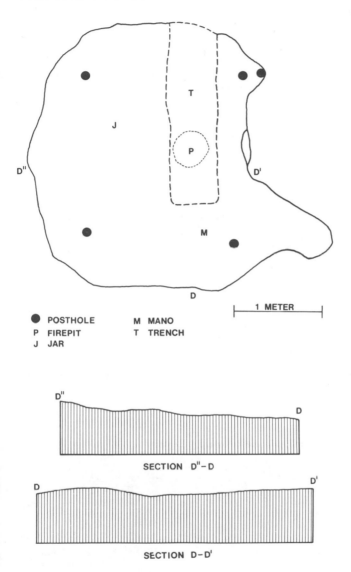

Figure 10.4. The Gurley sites: Pithouse Y.

and jars were all used exclusively for storage, would have provided about 1/10 m³ of storage space. By way of contrast, a single storage pit excavated in Area W, a limited-activity area near Pithouse X, would have provided 3–4 m³ of storage space. A single posthole in the bottom of this pit may indicate some type of a lean-to covering. But, the existence of storage space in any way analogous to a pueblo storage room seems unlikely at the Gurley sites.

Comparing outdoor activity space at the County Road and Gurley sites was somewhat difficult. In general, however, work space seems to have been somewhat more functionally specific at the Gurley sites. Table 10.3 shows the distribution of stone tools among the different houses, the activity spaces near the houses, and activity areas away from the houses. The figures are for all levels and show general differences between areas, rather than what was going on on particular surfaces. The figure shows that chipped stone tools were heavily concentrated in Area Z. Area Z was an activity area about 20 m from Pithouse Y and 60 m from Pithouse X. No more 2-m squares were excavated in this area than in any other. Cores also tended to be concentrated in this area and in Area W, a second limited-activity area about 40 m from Pithouse X. Manos and metates, on the other hand, were associated either with houses or activity space in the immediate vicinity of houses.

Table 10.4 focuses on the space closer to houses at the County Road and Gurley sites. The figure was created in the following manner. Each 2-m square at the sites was classified on the basis of whether it contained scrapers, cores, knives, manos, or some combination of these four artifact types. I chose these particular types because they represent a range of diversity in artifacts: Scrapers have steep edges; knives have acute ones; cores are debris from tool manufacture; and manos are used in grinding.

TABLE 10.3
Percentage Distribution of Artifacts by Area, All Levels

Artifact type	Pithouse 1	Pithouse 2	Pithouse X	Pithouse Y	Area I–II	Area X	Area Y	Area Z	Area W	Area U–V	Total (%)
Scrapers	6.4	7.2	4.5	0.0	11.1	5.4	0.0	48.0	10.9	5.8	100
Knives	7.4	2.2	5.1	2.2	13.5	4.8	5.8	40.0	12.9	7.8	100
Drills	30.0	0.0	0.0	0.0	0.0	0.0	0.0	60.0	10.0	0.0	100
Projectile points	30.4	0.0	8.7	0.0	4.4	13.0	8.7	21.6	8.7	4.4	100
Becs	8.9	6.7	2.2	0.0	8.9	8.9	0.0	46.7	15.6	2.2	100
Platform modification	4.5	0.0	3.0	0.0	4.5	10.5	0.0	49.5	21.0	7.5	100
Cores	8.3	1.2	5.9	1.2	15.6	11.3	5.9	34.6	12.2	2.8	100
Manos	38.0	0.0	14.0	2.0	0.0	16.0	14.0	4.0	10.0	2.0	100
Metates	37.5	0.0	0.0	0.0	0.0	25.0	12.5	0.0	12.5	12.5	100

TABLE 10.4
Artifact Combinations on the County Road and Gurley Sites

A. *Percentage of squares accounted for by artifact combinations*

	Site	
Artifact combination	County road site (%)	Gurley sites (%)
One artifact type	47.9	58.8
Two artifact types	37.5	20.6
Three artifact types	14.6	20.6
Four artifact types	00.0	00.0
Total	100.0	100.0

B. *Percentage of artifacts accounted for by each combination*

	Site	
Artifact combination	County road site (%)	Gurley sites (%)
One artifact type	22.4	32.8
Two artifact types	49.2	26.8
Three artifact types	28.3	40.4
Four artifact types	00.0	00.0
Total	100.0	100.0

C. *Percentage of artifacts accounted for by each combination with correction for the number of artifacts in an associational unit*

	Site	
Artifact combination	County road site (%)	Gurley sites (%)
One artifact type	39.5	54.4
Two artifact types	44.7	23.5
Three artifact types	15.7	22.2
Four artifact types	00.0	00.0
Total	100.0	100.0

In Table 10.4, I distinguished between squares that had only one type of artifact, squares that had a combination of two types, squares with a combination of three types, and squares with all four types. The table shows that from the County Road to the Gurley sites the percentage of squares that were the locus of only one artifact type increased. To check these results, I looked at the percentage of artifacts, not squares, accounted for by each of these combinations. Again, there was an increase in the percentage associated with the single artifact type. As an intermediate approach, I examined the percentage of associational units in each combination. An associational unit in the case of a single artifact type is one, two for a combination of two, and so on. In other words, the total number of artifacts associated with each combination was divided by the number of artifacts required to make a unit of association. Again, the Gurley sites appear to have been somewhat more functionally specific.

Summary

Data permitting the evaluation of the proposition that differentiation of activities occurred during the transition were sought, both within and between sites. Specifying a precise set of conditions for accepting or rejecting this proposition was difficult. Thus, the test implications contained both predictions concerning quantifiable trends and predictions of general differences between the two cultures.

1. The rate of increase in the area of utilized space employed as limited-activity sites should increase at a maximum during the transition period and reach an absolute maximum.
2. Diversity in representation of different kinds of limited-activity sites should be at a maximum during the transition period.
3. The topographical location of these sites should indicate that maximum diversity in the use of such situations occurs with the transition.
4. Within sites, specialization, viewed in terms of functionally specific architecture, should increase with the transition.
5. Unit-to-unit variability in the distribution of artifacts should be greater in Pueblo culture than in Basketmaker.

The total amount of utilized space employed as limited-activity sites increased three times over during the transition. After such sites appeared, this increase was the most rapid ever. Moreover, for A.D. 700–1200, the ratio of limited-activity site space to habitation-site space was low. Between A.D. 800–900, during the heart of the transition, this ratio was 1 : 1. Thus, the transition was associated with maximum increase and maximum utilization of limited-activity sites.

At A.D. 700, the coefficient of variability for limited-activity sites began to decrease. For the period A.D. 900–1000, the statistic was below .50. This means that of the different types of limited-activity sites defined, all but a few were represented and these tended to be represented fairly equally. Higher statistics outside this period indicate either that many of the types of sites were not present or that only a few of the types were heavily utilized. Diversity in the presence of limited-activity sites reached a maximum during the transition period.

Diversification in the use of topographical situations was examined in order to evaluate the relationship between differentiation and energy sources. Since topographical variation encompasses some quantity of variation in plant cover in this region, changes in this topographical index indicate changes and experimentation in resource exploitation. The statistic rose up to A.D. 900 and then dropped sharply. It was below .50 A.D. 900–1000 and remained relatively low until A.D. 1200. Again, these low figures indicate that most or all of the available topographical situations were being used and that they were being used with relatively comparable frequencies. In general, these changes were associated with a shift in habitation sites from the mesa tops to the valleys and in limited-activity sites from the valleys to the mesa tops. Changes in energy sources as reflected in topographical situations were apparently associated with the change from an adaptation that placed no primary value on the valley lands to one that heavily valued these lands, but continued to exploit the mountain sides intensively.

The discussion of differentiation within sites was primarily descriptive. Evidence suggesting significant differences with respect to activity differentiation is the following:

1. Functionally-specific storage rooms were associated with the Pueblo, but not the Basketmaker, adaptation.
2. Kivas appeared, first as a kind of functionally-specific space near the end of Basketmaker culture, and then as both functionally-specific and ritually-specific space in Pueblo culture.

3. There was greater room-to-room variability in artifacts associated with Pueblo culture than in Basketmaker. This suggests that different activities may have a complementary distribution within sites.

4. Specific classes of tools for making tools did in fact have a complementary distribution on the site examined. Tools for making ornaments occurred predominantly in one-half of the Pueblo, tools for making arrows in the other.

5. Outdoor activity space showed a greater tendency toward unifunctionality in late Basketmaker culture than earlier. The difference in the percentage of unifunctional activity squares on the two sites examined was significant at the .20 level. The difference in the percentage of associational units was significant at the .01 level. While no outdoor activity space for Pueblo sites was available for comparison, the trend probably continued.

All these data generally support the proposition that significant changes in the dimension of differentiation occurred during the transition. Furthermore, data supporting the existence of a link between technology and differentiation were presented.

CHAPTER ELEVEN

Changes in Social Organization

The study of the integration of prehistoric cultures is at once the oldest and the newest of archeological concerns. In one sense, archeology began in the palace and temple precinct. However, the object of archeologists who dug in such areas was more often extracting the contents than understanding the activities carried on there. More recently, archeologists have become interested in understanding the organizational structure of prehistoric adaptations. Deetz (1965), Longacre (1963), Hill (1965), Whallon (1965), and Leone (1968) have directed attention to integration and to the changing aspects of integration. These analyses have relied on changes in artifact style as basic data for inference.

In the particular case of the southwestern United States, a good deal of inference concerning prehistoric integration has centered on similarities between kivas and prehistoric structures with identical architectural morphology. In addition, the rich literature of Southwestern ethnography has led to the identification of prehistoric shrines and ritual paraphernalia. Several archeologists and anthropologists have examined the developmental history of the kiva (see Hawley 1950; Martin 1929; Vivian and Reiter 1960).

In analyzing changes in the integrative dimension, I originally defined three variables as critical: the structure of social groups, integration-specific architecture, and integration-specific roles.

Group Structure

The basic insights into the structure of local groups in the Upper Little Colorado were made by Longacre (1963) and Hill (1965). Each studied the distribution of design elements on painted pottery at pueblos in Hay Hollow Valley. Hill also studied stylistic variation in a variety of other artifacts. A nonrandom distribution of design elements at the Carter Ranch and at the Broken K sites was discovered. Some design elements were found to have a pan-village distribution. But a percentage of the design elements at each site was localized in restricted parts of the pueblos. This localization of design elements was used to infer the presence of residence groups within them.

At Carter Ranch, a site of about 16 habitation rooms, Longacre found two local groups. At Broken K, with about 40 habitation rooms, Hill found five residence groups. These five groups were organized in two larger groups, one of three units, and one of two units. Each of the local groups at Carter Ranch and at Broken K was associated with about eight habitation rooms. Hill (1965: 198) observes, "it would seem that Longacre's two units were equivalent to the smallest units defined at Broken K, and Carter Ranch site as a whole was equivalent to one of the major units at Broken K."

The evidence from Carter Ranch suggests that sites of its general size were the abode of family units split into two residence groups. At Broken K, the family units were differentiated at two levels. On one level, a family unit was associated with one of five residence groups. At a second level, these groups were opposed, with three of the local groups in one larger unit and two in the other. The sociological implications of this situation have been thoroughly discussed by Hill (1965).

The evidence obtained by Longacre and Hill concerning the organization of family units into one or more opposed local groups is basic to an analysis of changes in group structure. The number, eight, appears to be critical in this regard. About eight habitation units form a residence group, and the number of habitation rooms on a site seems to be in multiples of eight. I used this information to construct a typology for analyzing changing patterns of social structure in Hay Hollow Valley.

For each 50-year period in the history of the valley, I put each site into one of the following four size categories: 1 (Type A); 2–12 (Type B); 13–20 (Type C); and over 21 (Type D). This typology follows directly from the earlier discussion. Sites with only one room, often called field houses, were put in a distinct category. They may represent limited-activity sites, or the abode of a single family. Until further investigation offers some insight into this problem, such sites must be classified separately. A site with one local group would have up to 12 habitation rooms. Sites with fewer than 8 rooms may represent very small local groups, or they may represent a large extended family. Some one-group sites probably had a few more than 8 rooms. Defining sites with one local group as those with 2–12 habitation rooms allowed for variation. Sites with two local groups were those with 13–20 habitation rooms. Sites with more than 20 rooms were probably ones with distinction not only between local groups but between groups of local groups on the order of Broken K; they were generally of the same size as Broken K.

Given the test implications concerning group structure, the period A.D. 700–1000 in Hay Hollow Valley should be associated with an increase in the complexity of group structure, occurring at two levels. On one level, sites with many local groups should begin to replace single-group sites. At another level, the settlement pattern as a whole should become more balanced; that is, sites with different levels of complexity should tend to exist at the same time.

I examined the data from all four survey blocks of Hay Hollow Valley with these goals in mind. I investigated each 100-year period in the history of the valley, using two different initial points: in one instance, 100-year periods beginning at the century mark; and second, time periods beginning at the mid-century point. I found no significant differences between the two techniques. Four basic patterns of variation were isolated; Table 11.1 summarizes these data. The table shows the percentage of habitation rooms during successive 100-year time periods that fell into each of the size categories.

The first pattern of variation covered the period up to A.D. 600. During this period, a very high percentage of the rooms at any one time were on sites that fell into one size category. As explained earlier, the growth during this period was accounted for in terms of a few sites growing increasingly large. In general, 5% of the habitation rooms

TABLE 11.1
Percentage of Total Habitation Rooms on Each of Four Habitation Site Types

Time period (A.D.)	Site types (%)			
	A	B	C	D
200–250	17	83	0	0
250–300	0	100	0	0
300–350	0	100	0	0
350–400	0	20	37	43
400–450	0	10	0	90
450–500	0	10	0	90
500–550	5	36	27	32
550–600	1	54	45	0
600–650	11	44	45	0
650–700	12	88	0	0
700–750	8	73	19	0
750–800	10	90	0	0
800–850	3	81	16	0
850–900	5	40	36	19
900–950	8	40	52	0
950–1000	23	53	0	24
1000–1050	20	38	8	34
1050–1100	13	38	30	19
1100–1150	16	32	19	33
1150–1200	2	12	44	42
1200–1250	2	14	8	76
1250–1300	2	24	17	57
1300–1350	0	50	50	0
1350–1400	0	100	0	0
1400–1450	0	100	0	0

were on Type A sites; 50% on Type B; 20% on Type C; and 25% on Type D. But, the size of the dominant group varied considerably. Throughout this time range there was little indication of complexity on an intersite basis. During most of the 100-year periods, one size type accounted for more than 80% of the habitation rooms. For this reason, it did not seem likely that within sites of this period, complexity was great.

The second pattern of variation lasted from A.D. 600 to A.D. 850. During this period, very small sites, which did not exceed the level of a single local group, predominated. 9% of the habitation rooms were on Type A sites and 75% were on Type B sites. At the same time, there were few sites at the level of more than a single local group. Only 16% of the habitation rooms were on Type C sites and no Type D sites existed.

The third pattern of variation covered the period A.D. 950–1100. In this period, intersite complexity appeared. Table 11.1 shows that each site type accounted for a significant percentage of habitation rooms: Twenty-two percent of the habitation rooms were on Type A sites; 42% on Type B sites; 25% on Type C; and 19% on Type D. Furthermore, there was a greater representation of sites with multilocal group residence: Forty-four percent of the sites had more than one local group.

The final pattern, lasting from A.D. 1100 until the effective abandonment of the region at A.D. 1300, represented a maximum of intrasite complexity, with somewhat less intersite complexity. Sites with three or more local groups accounted for the majority (52%) of the habitation units during this period. The habitation rooms were distributed: Type A sites, 4%; Type B, 21%; and Type C, 22%. This pattern occurred during the span of time in which Hay Hollow Valley was being abandoned. Hill (1965) has partially demonstrated that the kind of agglomeration represented by Broken K is a response to dire environmental conditions. It does seem likely that a breakdown in organization at the intersite level was associated with increasing intrasite organization during this period.

In summary, the peak of complexity at both intrasite and intersite levels was achieved at about A.D. 1000. The immediately preceding period was one in which small group settlements with one or fewer residence groups predominated. Significantly, it was during this time span that Leone's (1968) measure of social autonomy reached a maximum (see also Connor, 1968). Small farming villages were indeed basic in the valley during this period. This same pattern seems to characterize the entire region (Longacre 1966. 96). The succeeding period was one that saw an increase in complexity within a few very large villages but a slight breakdown in intersite settlement pattern. One-group, two-group, and three-or-more group villages were all present in significant quantities, A.D. 850–1100. It is evident, then, that complexity measured in intrasite and intersite terms underwent its greatest increase A.D. 850–1100, during the period of transition from Basketmaker to Pueblo culture.

Architecture and Integration

One of the valuable sources of insight into changing patterns of integration in the prehistoric Southwest is the kiva. The kiva as an architectural unit is recognizable in prehistoric contexts, and the morphological continuity with historic kivas is great. Thus, changes in integration can be inferred to the extent that they reflected in their architectural component, the kiva.

The basic kind of evidence archeologists have used in inferring patterns of integration from kiva architecture is the relationship between kivas and other kinds of architectural units—habitation and storage rooms. Julian Steward (1937: 96–99) pointed to such basic changes in rooms that occurred with the transition to Pueblo culture.

Steward identified the appearance of the kiva with developmental Pueblo culture and the development of clan organization. He analyzed variation in the ratio of kivas to secular rooms over time. The following averages summarize his findings.

Pueblo I	1 : 6
Pueblo II	1 : 6
Pueblo III	1 : 14
Pueblo IV	1 : 60
Pueblo V	1 : 100

These figures represent the average ratio between kivas and secular rooms for the sites that Steward studied. At each succeeding level of cultural complexity, there were more secular rooms for each kiva. Steward associated this pattern with changes in the scope of integration; more and more secular units were associated with a single kiva, a single integrative locus. These conclusions have been accepted by other anthropologists (see Eggan 1950: 198–200; Hill 1965: 238; Longacre 1963: 125–126; Wendorf 1956: 19–20). The data certainly agree with the results obtained in discussing changing patterns of group organization in Hay Hollow Valley.

However, Steward's analysis did not deal with variation in the ratio of kivas to storage and habitation rooms at a single point in time. Such variation is substantial. In Mesa Verde, for example, Cliff Palace, Spruce Tree House, and Balcony House are Pueblo III sites. The ratio of kivas to secular rooms at each of these sites is, respectively, 1 : 7, 1 : 12.5, and 1 : 20. I do not believe that this variation among contemporaneous sites contradicts Steward's point. He discussed long-term variation, and averages are appropriate for this purpose. But, the variation that exists at a given point in time suggests there is a good deal of explaining still to be done.

Karl Polanyi has suggested that the transition to an agricultural economy might have been accompanied by a shift from a predominantly reciprocal to a predominantly redistributive mode of exchange (Polanyi 1957: 254). Does this argument provide insight into the variation in the ratio of kivas to secular rooms? If a redistributive exchange system appeared with agriculture, then one would expect it to be associated with existing pan-village institutions, in this case, the kiva. By the same token, if kivas acquired a redistributive function, storage rooms—the architectural evidence of the function of storing—should come to be associated with kivas. That is, storage should be handled by a pan-village institution, rather than a family one. There is evidence indicating that the function of storing changes from a family to a village activity. Available data suggest the following:

1. The initial appearance of kivas recognized as such represents a shift in activity loci in which a functionally specific pithouse acquires integrative functions.
2. The ratio of secular rooms to kivas in Pueblo III culture is double that in Pueblo II culture. At this time, kivas may acquire a redistributive function, at least a central storage one. .
3. The kiva-secular-room ratio in Pueblo IV culture is four times that in Pueblo III culture. This difference probably represents not an organizational change but a shift in the data that Steward used from the Chaco, Mesa Verde, and Kayenta areas to the Hopi and Rio Grande Pueblos.

Many anthropologists have considered the origin of kivas. Martin (1929), in one detailed analysis of kiva history, has suggested that they were derived from subterranean houses. Several lines of evidence support this reasoning. In the first place, kivas are, by and large, pithouses. A kiva is a room, usually subterranean, with a roof entrance, a firepit, a ventilator, some wall niches, and a bench or platform along one or more of the walls. Long after below-ground, circular structures have ceased to be the typical Southwestern dwelling unit, structures that are circular and below ground survive in the form of kivas.

Kivas are not simply pithouses. Martin (1929: 35) has suggested

that at the Basketmaker, and perhaps even Pueblo I, level of organization, specialized kinds of activities were carried on in these rooms.
He associated these activities with ones that would be carried on in
a men's house.

Unfortunately, no excavations have been undertaken with this idea
in mind. For most of the Southwest it is difficult or impossible to
evaluate Martin's hypothesis. During the summer of 1968, however,
two subterranean structures were excavated by the Expedition that
shed some light on the problem. These structures were described
in Chapter 10. To summarize what has already been said, the structures had the architectural attributes of kivas. The artifact assemblage
from each structure was different from that which one would associate
with a habitation room or even a general purpose activity area. Manos,
metates, and pottery were relatively absent. Worked slabs, cores, and
unutilized flakes were present in considerable numbers. The manufacture of stone tools seemed to be localized in the structures. A spindle
whorl, a cloudblower, and remnants of necklaces or bracelets were
found in one structure.

In short, the structures had the architectural attributes of kivas,
but artifactually they seemed to have served primarily as a place where
stone tools were made. Ethnographically, the manufacture of stone
tools is almost exclusively a male activity. The kiva, then, was the
locus of a very specialized set of activities usually performed by men.

One of the kivas stood alone. It was not associated with a typical
dwelling unit. The second kiva was adjacent to Pithouse 1, also discussed previously and identified as a habitation unit. Pithouse 1 and
the adjacent kiva are probably contemporaneous. (Carbon-14 and
tree-ring dates are given in Appendix II.) A similar association of
a pithouse with a single kiva was excavated at the Reidhead Site in
1964. At present, however, there is no way to verify whether this
pattern is representative of the Southwest as a whole. Shallow houses
associated with deep, kiva-like structures have been reported from
Mesa Verde (Lancaster et al. 1954: 7); but, so little attention has been
paid to living floors that data are generally unavailable for discovering
whether the pattern that emerges from the Reidhead and Gurley
sites is typical.

If the pattern is representative, then it suggests that at one time
the ratio of kivas to secular units may have been 1 : 1. Specific kinds
of activities, but not necessarily integrative ones, were carried on in

kivas. In Pueblo culture, more and more rooms were associated with a single kiva, and the kiva seems to have taken on integrative functions. In modern pueblo culture, it certainly serves this purpose. Evidence from Broken K Pueblo (Hill 1965: 39) and from the literature of contemporary Pueblo culture (Mindeleff 1891: 130) suggests that there is a residue of men's house activities associated with kivas in both early and modern Pueblo groups.

Basic changes in kiva activities are associated with classic Pueblo culture. These changes probably began to occur around A.D. 1000 and were complete by A.D. 1100–1300. In Steward's (1937) analysis, the number of rooms associated with each kiva doubled at this time, and the place of the kiva in the village architectural pattern also changed. For the period A.D. 800–1000, kivas were generally located outside the block of habitation and storage rooms. Later, they come to be a more integral part of the room block. Great kivas, 5–20 times the size of room kivas, also appeared with Pueblo II culture.

This change is associated with a change in the pattern that relates habitation rooms, storage rooms, and kivas. Prior to A.D. 1000, habitation and storage rooms were adjacent to each other, and kivas were separate. After this date, kivas were associated with some storage rooms, while other storage rooms continued to be contiguous to habitation rooms. Three different sets of architectural data point to this pattern.

In the period A.D. 1100–1300, a group of structures referred to in the literature as tri-wall structures appeared. These consisted of a kiva surrounded by two rings of rooms. The rooms were small, about 6 m², and on that basis were likely to have been storage rooms. Furthermore, the rooms usually lacked any features, and few artifacts were found on the floors. Vivian (1959: 85) has suggested that they might have been rooms in which the ritual paraphernalia of an incipient priestly class was stored. Vivian identified such structures at Aztec (2), Chaco Canyon (2), the Mancos Valley in Colorado, the McElmo Valley, and northwestern New Mexico (2). Peckham's (1962) Red Willow Site is a bi-wall, a kiva surrounded by a single ring of rooms. Fire Temple and Sun Temple at Mesa Verde are structures in which kivas were associated with a number of small rooms (Fewkes 1916; Vivian and Reiter 1964).

In short, an architectural entity appeared in which a kiva was associated with one or more rings of storage rooms. Habitation rooms did not occur in these structures. They were usually nearby, but not contiguous with the tri-walls. In the combination of kivas and storage rooms, these structures associated integrative with storage activities.

At about this same time, great kivas appeared. Great kivas also seem to have had peripheral rooms that on the basis of the attributes examined are typologically storage rooms. This pattern is not conclusive because data that would allow a firm judgment were, by and large, unavailable.

In most instances when archeologists have excavated outside the walls of a great kiva, peripheral rooms have been found. In the Upper Little Colorado, this pattern was evident at Hooper Ranch (Martin *et al.* 1962), Carter Ranch (Martin *et al.* 1964), and Site 201 (Zubrow 1971a,b). Elsewhere in the Southwest, Aztec, Casa Rinconada, Chetro Ketl I, Pueblo Bonito I, Pueblo Bonito III, and Lowry Pueblo are examples (Vivian and Reiter 1960). Because excavators chose not to investigate what lay beyond the kiva walls, there is no evidence as to whether this pattern characterizes other great kivas. It is amazing that archeologists who have been quick to see potential storage space in every nook and cranny of a great kiva have generally not excavated beyond their walls when, since the 1930s, evidence of rooms outside the walls has been present. For the great kivas mentioned above, it was possible to determine whether there were peripheral rooms, and in every case there were.

A final set of data bearing on the relationship between integration and storage concerns the smaller, or room, kivas. These kivas are of the type that prior to about A.D. 1000 were located outside the room block and afterward were located inside. A.D. 1100–1300, room blocks were composed of a unit in which the kiva was at the center, surrounded by a row of storage rooms in turn surrounded by a row of habitation rooms. Block A at Village of the Great Kivas (Roberts 1932) and Lowry Pueblo both show this pattern of construction. In sites of the period A.D. 1100–1300 in the Upper Little Colorado, Mesa Verde and Chaco Canyon, 15–50% of storage rooms on sites were associated with kivas in the manner described above. The units could have been constructed in such a way that the kivas were adjacent only to habitation rooms. They were not. Nevertheless, there was so much intersite variation in this pattern, that it is the weakest of the lines of evidence presented.

It does, however, offer some insight into the problem with which I initially began: Why do three contemporaneous sites in Mesa Verde have such very different ratios of kivas to secular rooms? The answer may be that sites with great numbers of kivas were redistributive centers of some sort. Sites like Cliff Palace, with seven secular rooms for each kiva, and Village of the Great Kivas, with a 1:6 ratio, also had an inordinately large number of storage rooms. Cliff Palace had 1.25 storage rooms for each habitation room. In comparison, Spruce Tree House had only 0.33.

To summarize, the activity of storing was becoming centralized. It was associated with kivas in tri-wall structures. Great kivas had a series of peripheral rooms that were probably storage rooms. Sites with large numbers of kivas also had large numbers of storage rooms. Storage was handled in some part by a pan-village or even a pan-regional group. The existence of centralized storage facilities may mean that a redistributive system of some sort was in operation.

This argument conflicts with what we know of kiva functions in the present. Storage is not handled centrally, and redistribution scarcely exists. Moreover, there are no regional storage centers. That Pueblo culture has no such organization in the present is not firm basis for concluding that it did not in the past.

In the first place, Steward's scope of integration continued to increase after A.D. 1300: But it did not increase due to indigenous developments. Mesa Verde, Chaco Canyon, and northeastern Arizona, the regions from which Steward's data were drawn in describing Pueblo II and Pueblo III culture, were abandoned. The figures that he used for Pueblo IV and V were drawn from Hopi and Rio Grande pueblos.

These areas were not abandoned. Environmentally, they were more secure than the remainder of the Southwest because of more favorable environmental conditions (Hack 1942: 79). Furthermore, both regions had irrigation and other water control systems. Yearly crop failures were not as likely as elsewhere, and redistribution as a protection against famine may never have become important. Cooperation was probably focused more on water control systems than on redistribution (Eggan 1966: 318–319). The latter does a good deal more to protect an adaptation from some environments.

Burial Populations and Roles

If kivas acquired a redistributive function, then one would expect that a group of integrative functionaries might also have come into existence. Vivian (1959) associated tri-wall structures and the appearance of a complex settlement organization in Chaco Canyon with an incipient priestly class. Again, there is little evidence of such stratification in modern Pueblo organization. But, it would be consistent with the discussion thus far if such a high-status group had existed in the prehistoric Southwest.

In fact, Vivian has collected a substantial quantity of data suggesting that the social organization in Chaco Canyon was quite complex. Decades ago, most archeologists believed that the small, crudely built pueblos on the west side of Chaco Wash were Pueblo I, while towns such as Pueblo Bonito, on the east side, were Pueblo II and III. Tree-ring dates from the area have made this position untenable. The adaptations to the two sides of the wash are contemporaneous, but their material culture is quite distinct.

The east, or town, side of the wash has preconceived floor plans, veneered, decorated masonry, kivas, great kivas, tower kivas, tri-walled structures, turquoise jewelry and mosaics, carved stone and wood, copper bells, parrots, macaws, irrigation canals, dams, reservoirs, and field grids. The west, or village, side of the wash is associated with random, irregular floor plans, no veneering or decoration of masonry, room kivas only, no jewelry, carved stone, or decorative or trade items such as those found on the east side of the wash and no water control or field systems (Vivian and Mathews 1964: 109). The differences between the two adaptations are surely not seasonal or ecological as the two types of sites are only a few hundred yards apart: The difference must be organizational. However, none of Vivian's data speaks to the existence of a priestly class per se.

Unfortunately, analytic techniques have outstripped available data in the study of roles. But archeologists have inferred role patterns from prehistoric data, specifically burial data. J. C. Gardin (1965b) suggested that a formal or componential analysis of burial populations would allow archeologists to infer something of the roles played by individuals and something of the role structure of a population. This principle has been applied by Brown (1966) to the burial population from Spiro mound, by Merbs (1968) to Artic populations, and by Saxe (1968) to ethnographic data.

Saxe has described the principles underlying such analyses. He begins with two terms—social identity and social persona. A social identity refers to a category of persons, a social position. A social persona is a grammatically possible combination of social identities selected for interaction on a given occasion. Saxe (1968: 4–5) then notes that,

> In differently organized societies, different identities vary as to the number of identity relationships that is grammatically possible for them to have . . . if we were to find infants buried with the accoutrement of a social persona larger than some elders, a principle of social ranking by birth is probably indicated. In egalitarian societies such a combination of age and accoutrement would be "ungrammatical" i.e., syntactically impossible.

Different social persona with different sets of grammatically possible social identities are subject to different mortuary treatment. When we excavate burial populations, we are able to study mortuary practices. Employing the assumptions explained by Saxe and the techniques used by Brown, Merbs, and Saxe, some elements of social structure can be inferred.

Unfortunately, the data upon which such analyses might be made are generally unavailable. Burial populations from late prehistoric Pueblo times are rare. The populations that have been excavated are usually not reported in terms amenable to this type of analysis. Measurements of bones are reported, but not age, sex, orientation or burial furnishings.

Nevertheless, a limited amount of information is available. A list of 231 burials from 14 sites was compiled in part by Straus (1968), during the 1968 Expedition field season and is shown in Table 11.2. In this analysis, burials are defined as high status on the basis of the inclusion of either unusual burial furniture or large quantities of furnishings relative to the other burials. In some instances, the unique aspects of the burial were noted by the investigator and in other cases by Straus or Plog.

The pattern is a definitive one. Of the 82 burials associated with pithouse villages, 3, or 4%, are high-status burials. Of 148 burials associated with pueblo sites, 37, or 25%, of the burials fall into this category. In other words, one-fourth of the burial population was treated in a deferential manner.

This picture generally agrees with a detailed analysis of burial populations at the Carter Ranch site (Longacre 1963). Longacre noted that 9 of the 34 burials on the site were different from the others. The bodies were buried in the center of the burial area, had almost all of the unusual grave furnishings, and had extraordinarily high

TABLE 11.2
High-Status Burials[a]

Site	High-status burials	Total burials
Pithouse sites		
Bluff	0	2
Bear	0	40
Site 30	0	1
Cerro Colorado	2	14
Shabik'eschee	1	15
Alkali Ridge 13	0	7
Total	3	79
Pueblo sites		
Site 31	2	2
Carter Ranch	10	34
Mesa Verde 499	3	8
Mineral Creek	3	5
Mesa Verde 866	3	11
Broken K	2	2
Mesa Verde 34	8	36
Higgins Flat	6	15
Total	37	113

[a] After Straus 1968.

quantities of pottery and design elements on the pottery that were unique. The design elements associated with the remaining burials were the same as one or the other of the local groups at the pueblo.

A pattern indicating even more role differentiation is evident at Grasshopper Pueblo, now being excavated by the University of Arizona Field School (Griffin 1967). A group of burials with all the qualitative and quantitative attributes of high status are buried in the main plaza next to the kiva. Ordinary burials occur in the fields outside the pueblo proper. Most significant, there are infant and child burials in the high-status group. Apparently, by the time that Grasshopper was occupied, there were high-status roles into which an individual could be born.

Unfortunately, it is impossible to go beyond these provocative suggestions of differentiation. One can only hope that burial populations will be more frequently discovered and more rigorously analyzed in the future.

Summary

Evaluating change in the dimension of integration during the transition was difficult. Three sets of data were examined in considering the proposition that significant changes in this dimension are associated with the transition.

1. The Group Structure of Settlements. The available evidence indicated that the transition was associated with an increase in the number of sites with more than one local residence group. Large sites were associated with the population maximum of Basketmaker culture, but there is as yet no evidence suggesting that the large aggregates of people had complex integrative institutions. The maximum of complexity associated with the transition occurred at an intersite, as well as an intrasite, level. During and after the transition, there tended to be a good representation of different types of local residence group arrangements. A maximum of intrasite and intersite complexity was reached about A.D. 1000. Maximum intrasite complexity was reached later, but then intersite complexity had begun to deteriorate.

2. The Appearance of New Architectural Structures Associated with Integration. Several lines of evidence suggested that the appearance of great kivas and other complex architectural forms also represented significant change in kiva function. The function of storage came to be associated with the kiva. The data supporting this conclusion were peripheral rooms around kivas, storage rooms around kivas in tri-wall structures, and an apparent tendency for sites with large numbers of kivas to also have large numbers of storage rooms. These data suggested that the kiva may have acquired a redistributive function. Data previously presented concerning tools for making tools in an apparent complementary distribution also supported this inference. In any case, central storage appeared and was associated with the kiva. To the extent that such a system protected individual families, lineages, or villages from famine, by providing food or seed for planting, it represents a clear increase in the stability of the subsistence base, a link between the dimensions of integration and technology.

3. Role Differentiation. An analysis of several burial populations suggested that Pueblo culture was associated with a more differentiated burial complex than is Basketmaker culture. The difference between the two is significant at the .01 level. So few burials received special treatment in the Basketmaker culture that those that did could be attributed to chance. For Pueblo culture this was not the case. In fact, evidence from Grasshopper Pueblo suggested that role differentiation had proceeded to a point where ascribed integrative roles existed. Increasing role differentiation suggests increasingly complex integrative mechanisms and forges the link between the dimensions of differentiation and integration. The general process of differentiation that occurred during the transition appears to have had its specific consequence in the differentiation of integrative roles.

CHAPTER TWELVE

Technological Change

The Basketmaker–Pueblo transition as defined by Kidder (1927) can be characterized by a number of technological changes, which were discussed in Chapter 3 of this volume. Let us now turn to a consideration of the occurrence of these changes in the Upper Little Colorado and Hay Hollow Valley. One may characterize the adoption of an innovation in a variety of different ways: determining the date of first appearance of the adoption, determining the point at which the rate of adoption of the innovation becomes a high one (i.e., the inflexion point), or creating a general graph of the abundance of the innovation at a number of points in time. This last approach is of course the best, since it includes information on the first two. Unfortunately, it is not always possible to obtain data amenable to this treatment. Therefore, in considering the record of adoption of innovations in the area, I will list what I take to be the points of initial appearance and the inflexion points for each of two technological innovations that are critical to the transition, and I will provide continuous data for three innovations that are sufficiently well described to permit this form of analysis.

Agriculture. While corn is not strictly speaking a technological innovation, it is an important innovation. And since there is no possibility
of fully evaluating changes in resources for the reasons discussed
earlier, we will consider this change here. The earliest site in Hay
Hollow Valley with evidence of the practice of agriculture is the County
Road site which dates to roughly 1000 B.C. Given that agricultural
products are in use at least 1000 years earlier in other areas of the
Southwest, one might assume that this date would be even earlier
if we were able to excavate the kind of dry caves from which such
evidence is typically obtained. For now, however, we must use the
date of 1000 B.C. The date at which a rapid adoption of this subsistence
strategy began is somewhat difficult to establish. Agricultural products
were found at the Hay Hollow site, and the Gurley sites. At the former,
the role of such resources in the diet was apparently still minimal
as only two fragments were found. Agriculture was clearly more
important by A.D. 500–600, when the Gurley sites were occupied,
although the evidence suggests that gathered products still constituted
the major portion of the diet.

Hevly's (1964) study of the presence of pollen from cultivated plants
in archeological sites begins at about A.D. 500. From this point, and
over the next 100 years, the importance of these pollens was in decline.
In the late 600s, the percentages for both cultivated and noncultivated
economic pollens increased, but again declined after A.D. 700. From
the late 800s, until A.D. 1100, Hevly has only a very limited amount
of data. However, it is clear from my own work that by A.D. 1000,
populations were beginning to practice irrigation and other water
control strategies in the valley. Palynological evidence indicates that
corn and cucurbits were grown in the fields that these canals watered
(Dickey 1971). Thus, the beginning of a reasonably rapid change
to a reliance on agricultural products must have begun around A.D.
700–900. An important change in the variety of corn used in the area
occurred at about A.D. 950. A corn with 12–14 rows and small cupules
was replaced by a variety with only 8 rows and much larger cupules
(Cutler 1964: 228). Cutler (1952: 469) has argued that the second
variety of corn is better adapted to an arid climate, such as that of the
Southwest. Thus, an increase in the security and perhaps productivity
of this resource is implied.

No argument is implied here that local population were evolving
in the direction of a fully agricultural society. As Hevly's (1964) data
rather clearly indicate, gathered products remained important

throughout the prehistoric sequence in the area. And, I shall later argue that for this reason, one may wish to regard agriculture as a temporary experiment that failed.

Pottery. Pottery was in use in the Upper Little Colorado no later than A.D. 200 at the Hay Hollow site. Black-on-white pottery was used at the Gurley sites in the sixth and seventh centuries A.D. Corrugated forms were present in the valley no later than A.D. 950 and no earlier than about A.D. 850. Again, because of the dearth of dry caves, nothing is known of the relative decline in basketry through these periods. However, the Gurley sites are the first in which pottery is present in sufficient quantities that one might imagine pottery, rather than baskets, were the primary containers used by the local populations.

Architecture. Pithouse sites in the valley and the region were occupied as late as about A.D. 900. The earliest date for pueblo architecture is also at about A.D. 900. This particular innovation is one that was adopted very rapidly. Even guessing that there may be somewhat earlier pueblo sites and somewhat later pithouse sites would leave us believing the transition covered a period no longer than A.D. 800–1000.

Storage. The change from storage pits to storage rooms was essentially coterminous with the shift from pithouses to pueblos.

Manos and Metates. The shift from basin to trough metates occurred before the beginning of the Christian era; 80% of the metates from the Hay Hollow site were trough metates, although slab metates were also present by this time. But, there is no evidence of a significant pattern of adoption of these artifacts until A.D. 500–600, when the Gurley sites were occupied, and slab metates did not become important until the time of occupation of the Carter Ranch site, about A.D. 950.

Atlatl to Bow and Arrow. Most Southwestern archeologists are not speaking of physical atlatls and bows and arrows when they discuss this transition. The number of these artifacts that have been recovered is minute. What we usually have in mind is the transition from long, thick projectile points, which we associate with atlatls, to shorter, thinner projectile points, which we associate with the bow and arrow. To the extent that this equation is a workable one, atlatls were the exclusive throwing implement present at the Hay Hollow site. At

TABLE 12.1
The Occurrence of Innovations

Artifact	Earliest date	Inflexion point of adoption curve
Corn	1000 B.C.	A.D. 700–900
Pottery	A.D. 200	A.D. 600
Black-on-white	A.D. 500	A.D. 850
Corrugated	A.D. 850	A.D. 900
Architecture	A.D. 800	A.D. 900
Storage	A.D. 800	A.D. 900
Metates		
(trough to slab)	A.D. 200	A.D. 800
Projectile points	A.D. 200	A.D. 500

the Gurley sites, approximately 50% of each form of artifact was present; and by A.D. 850, when the Hatch site was occupied, nearly all of the projectile points were of the smaller, thinner variety.

Table 12.1 summarizes the data concerning the record of technological innovation in the valley, again including agriculture. Two points should be clear. First, most of the tool forms were present in the area for a substantial period of time before they were actually adopted. Second, the adoption of innovation in general tended to be concentrated in the period A.D. 800–1000.

It is possible to examine the record of adoption of innovation using a continuous record of change for four items: storage pits, projectile points, manos, and metates.

Storage

Storage is a variable that measures both changes in resource availability and changes in the efficiency of a productive system. Data concerning storage space in the Upper Little Colorado were collected by Zilen (1968). These data are summarized in Table 12.2. The raw data with which Zilen dealt were storage pits in the case of the Basketmaker adaptation and storage rooms in the case of the Pueblo. In evaluating the Pueblo data, a height of 1 m above the floor was used in defining effective storage space. The data in Table 12.2 show the increase in the volume of storage space per dwelling unit at each site.

TABLE 12.2
Storage Space Per Habitation Unit in the Upper Little Colorado[a]

Site	Date (circa)	Storage space per dwelling unit (m³)
County Road	70 B.C.	0.14
Hay Hollow	A.D. 60	0.33
Site 30	A.D. 700	0.28
Gurley	A.D. 700	0.80
Mineral Creek	A.D. 950	4.25
Rim Valley	A.D. 1000	5.28
Carter Ranch	A.D. 1050	6.83
Broken K	A.D. 1200	4.78
Hooper Ranch	A.D. 1250	5.93
Table Rock	A.D. 1350	5.17

[a]After Zilen 1968.

Tools

The original definition of the Basketmaker–Pueblo transition was based upon technological changes—changes in architecture, projectile points, containers, etc. In this section, I hope to show that these changes are not random variations in the morphology of artifacts or style changes, but, rather, changes in the efficiency of manufacture or use of those artifacts.

For example, Ford (1968: 2–3) linked changes in containers with changes in nutrition. He argued that when corn is cooked in water, the amount of starch that is available for conversion to glucose nearly doubles. Since pottery holds water and can be used as a cooking utensil, its invention would substantially increase the nutritive value of the diet of a group that ate corn, even if the variety or abundance of corn remained constant.

If the transition from Basketmaker to Pueblo was an economic transformation, then technological innovation should have occurred during this transition. Projectile points, on the one hand, and manos and metates, on the other, might have played critical roles. Projectile points are used in hunting and manos and metates in processing vegetal products. Since the importance of hunting was declining, hunting tools would be expected to become less important. A production process that requires less time and energy might have appeared, even if it resulted in more standardized, less specialized, forms of projectile points. With respect to manos and metates, changes might be expected in the opposite direction. The processes of manufacturing the tools might be more complex, but more specialized kinds cf tools should result.

Changes in these artifacts were analyzed during the 1968 Expedition field season. Traugott (1968) examined in detail changes in 120 projectile points from several sites in Hay Hollow Valley. He demonstrated that the process of manufacturing projectile points became more efficient and the product more standardized.

There were two processes of projectile point manufacture in the valley. The first predominated until about A.D. 750. There were four steps in this process of projectile point manufacture:

1. Removal of the projectile point blank from a core
2. Primary flaking to thin the blank
3. Secondary flaking to shape the blank
4. Heat treating the core or the blank—this step was observed in 60% of the specimens

The second process of projectile point manufacture, which predominated after A.D. 750, had only two steps: (1) the removal of a blank from a core and (2) secondary chipping to shape the point.

Two stages, primary flaking and heat treating, were no longer present in the second process. Since the more controlled flaking technique resulted in the removal of thinner blanks from the core, primary flaking was unnecessary. The importance of heat treating was also greatly diminished, with only 4% of the specimens showing evidence of it. In the sense that the second process involved fewer activities than the first, it was more efficient, and less stone was required to make a projectile point using the second process.

Furthermore, projectile points produced by the second process were more standardized than those produced by the first. The attribute of length illustrates this point. The mean length of projectile points made by process one is 39.5 mm, and the standard deviation is 10.4. Among points made by the second process, the mean is 22.8 mm, and the standard deviation, 5.7. The joint mean of the two groups is 31.1 mm. Variability in the first population is 33% and in the second, 18%. Thus, there was almost twice as much variability in projectile points made by the first process.

TABLE 12.3
Changes in the Process of Projectile Point Manufacture:
Hay Hollow Valley[a]

Site	Process I		Process II	
	Heat treated	Nonheat treated	Heat treated	Nonheat treated
Hay Hollow	20	7	0	0
Gurley	2	4	0	8
Hatch	1	1	1	30
Carter (I)	0	0	2	41
Carter (All)	1	4	2	41

[a] After Traugott 1968.

The changes in the importance of the two processes are evident in Table 12.3. At A.D. 100 (Hay Hollow site), all the points were made by the first process. At the Gurley sites (A.D. 700), 60% of the points were made by the first process. By A.D. 850 (Hatch site), only 40% of the points were made thus. All of the points Longacre (1964) believed indigenous to Carter Ranch were made by the second process. His distinction between indigenous and nonindigenous points, however, is essentially a distinction between points that are made by the second and the first processes, respectively. That is, Longacre believed that some of the points at Carter Ranch were morphologically too early to have been made at the site. In fact, Longacre simply may have been noting that the first manufacturing process was still present. Even if this interpretation is correct, it accounts for only 10–23% of the points. (Of the 48 points that Traugott examined, 5 were made by the first process. No more than 14 of 60 points could have been made by the first process.)

Parallel kinds of changes occurred in grinding tools. Early manos, for example, were simply ovate cobbles recognizable as manos only because of characteristic wear patterns. Later manos were thin and rectangular and were trimmed and shaped to a considerable extent. The major changes in the grinding tool complex affected the grinding surfaces. Less efficient surfaces were replaced by more efficient ones.

The effective grinding surface of a basin metate is a depression in the center of the metate. On trough metates, the effective grinding surface is limited only by ridges on two or three edges of the metate.

The actual grinding surface covers most of the top side of the metate. Finally, the entire surface of a slab metate comes into play in grinding. To the extent that basin metates were replaced by trough metates that were in turn replaced by slab metates (Martin and Rinaldo 1951), morphological changes were occurring in which the effective grinding surface, expressed as a percentage of the entire metate surface, increased.

Increases in the effective grinding surface of manos also occurred. Round manos are generally associated with basin metates. They are smaller than rectangular manos in order to fit the basin depression. Round manos were on the average 9 cm × 10 cm (based on 100 observations), while rectangular ones were 20 cm × 10 cm (based on 100 observations), with a few as large as 25 cm × 20 cm. Similarly, the effective grinding surface increased to the extent that manos with flat or beveled surfaces replaced manos with convex surfaces. The change from convexity to flatness increased the percentage of the grinding surface that was in contact with the metate at any point in time. Finally, efficiency increased to the extent that two-handed manos replaced one-handed ones. Not only did the effective grinding surface increase by 50% or more, but two hands, rather than one, could be used in conducting force to the mano.

These changes in mano and metate forms continually produced a more effective grinding surface. Burkenroad (1968) traced changes in these forms for nine sites in the Upper Little Colorado. He examined over 500 manos and 100 metates. The results are in Table 12.4. These results show a consistent pattern of change in each attribute except the convexity/flatness of mano surfaces. Trough metates predominated A.D. 100–700. After this time, they were present in quantities equal to the number of slab metates. At the latest site in the sample, slab metates accounted for 94% of the metates found. At about A.D. 800, rectangular manos began to predominate over round ones. Two hundred years earlier, two-handed metates had become more prevalent than one-handed ones. By A.D. 700 they were twice as common. The morphological changes in the direction of increasing efficiency were complete in all categories by A.D. 1000.

Summary

Strictly technological changes had a good deal to do with the Basketmaker–Pueblo transition. The process of manufacturing projectile

TABLE 12.4
Changes in Metate and Mano Attributes: Upper Little Colorado[a]

	Metates				Manos		
Site	Basin (%)	Trough (%)	Slab (%)	Total (%)	Round: rectangular ratio	1 hand: 2 hand ratio	Convex: flat ratio
Beach	100.0	0.0	0.0	100	12.0 : 1	0.0 : 1.	2.7 : 1
Hay Hollow	13.0	80.0	7.0	100	3.2 : 1	1.3 : 1	1.9 : 1
Mesa	18.0	79.0	3.0	100	1.8 : 1	1.4 : 1	0.7 : 1
Village	0.0	100.0	0.0	100	1.5 : 1	0.9 : 1	3.2 : 1
Gurley	12.5	75.0	12.5	100	1.3 : 1	0.5 : 1	0.4 : 1
Carter Ranch	5.0	47.5	47.5	100	0.1 : 1	0.2 : 1	0.6 : 1
Broken K	11.0	11.0	78.0	100	0.2 : 1	0.2 : 1	0.2 : 1
Foote Canyon	0.0	54.0	46.0	100	0.5 : 1	0.04 : 1	1.0 : 1
Table Rock	3.0	3.0	94.0	100	1.0 : 1	0.04 : 1	0.3 : 1

[a] After Burkenroad 1968.

points became simpler and the product more standardized. Hunting was apparently becoming less important. Specialized hunting tools would have been less necessary. Given these factors, as well as the increasing importance of agriculture and gathering, innovation in the direction of simplifying hunting tools and processes of making hunting tools occurred.

Manos and metates changed quite differently. There is no clear-cut evidence of change in tool manufacture. Increased time may have been spent in shaping manos, but this is not certain. A series of changes in the morphology of manos and metates that would have increased the grinding surface and efficiency in transmitting energy are clear. As gathering and agriculture became more important, innovations in the direction of increased efficiency in grinding tools occurred.

Finally, the quantity of storage space increased. Outdoor storage pits were replaced by indoor rooms. Below-ground storage was replaced by above-ground storage. These innovations increased the quantity of space available, the utility of the space, and, possibly, the security of storage.

It has been known for a long time that projectile points, manos, metates, and storage space underwent changes during the transition.

Usually, the changes have been regarded as stylistic or even random. This analysis has attempted to show that the changes that occurred involved evolution in the direction of increased efficiency either in tool production or tool use.

CHAPTER THIRTEEN

Summary and Conclusions

In this final chapter, I will attempt to identify what I regard as the achievements and limitations of this piece of research. It must be admitted at the outset that the research effort was neither a complete success nor a complete failure. Like most attempts to understand sociocultural phenomena, it was a mixture of the two. I will argue, however, that both in its success and in its failure, it pointed to new questions that must be pursued if we are to adequately understand phenomena such as the Basketmaker–Pueblo transition. In evaluating the research, I will focus primarily on two questions. (1) Did the research provide new information concerning the phenomenon under consideration? (2) Did the research provide a basis for understanding and explaining the phenomenon?

Information

The basic developmental sequence of Southwestern culture history covering the past 2000 years was defined by A. V. Kidder (1927) in the 1920s. Although this sequence has been defined somewhat differently by anthropologists using information that Kidder did not have, Kidder's fundamental concept of Basketmaker and Pueblo stages has been retained. Most of the work done after Kidder has been in a strictly defined space–time tradition. New traits, new tree-ring dates, new radiocarbon dates, and new evidence linking the appearance of new traits to other parts of the New World constitute the bulk of the additional knowledge obtained in the past 50 years. However, the cultural sequence that Kidder defined was neither explicitly spatial nor explicitly temporal. Kidder's intention was to characterize the development of prehistoric Southwestern cultures and to explain why and how the developments occurred. Few recent works have focused on this problem.

This research focused directly on attempting to explain the transition from Basketmaker to Pueblo culture. Moreover, it sought to understand this transition in such a way that models developed in the effort could be applied to similar periods of change, at other times and in other places. Primary emphasis was placed upon four phenomena: population, the organization of work, the integration of social activities, and technology. The discussion of the transition in terms of these four phenomena constituted new information, especially insofar as patterns of change that seem to underly the transition were identified. (No attempt will be made to generalize these changes for the entire Southwest. The data upon which such an effort might be based are substantially unavailable.)

In short, this analysis of the transition in terms of the identified patterns of cultural variability represents an addition to Kidder's analysis which focused principally on traits and trait complexes. It has identified the processual context in which these trait changes occurred.

Explanation

That new information concerning the transition has been obtained is of little consequence in and of itself. The important point concerns the extent to which this new information assists the archeologist in understanding and explaining the Basketmaker–Pueblo transition. *I do not claim to have offered a complete explanation of the transition, only to have made a first step in that direction.* What is the nature of this step? The question may be answered by reference to somewhat more specific questions about the transition as it has now been explicated.

(1) What has the discussion contributed to our understanding of the context in which the technological changes that define the transition occurred? (2) What has the discussion contributed to our understanding of causal relationships between changes in technology and in the dimensions of population, differentiation, integration, and energy?

The Context of the Transition

In an initial sense, the research offered an explanation for the transition by evaluating a series of arguments suggesting that specific events should occur in the context of other specified events. The primary event in which we were interested was the Basketmaker–Pueblo transition—the period of time during which the technological changes that Kidder observed occurred. The contextual events were set forth in the definition of growth—demographic change, changing work structure, organizational change, and changes in resources. We may first ask whether the transition, as Kidder defined it, occurred in the context of changes in these dimensions. At the same time, we must ask whether the relationships among the dimensions follow the pattern that was predicted in developing the growth model. In considering these topics, our focus for the Upper Little Colorado will be on the period A.D. 850–1050.

POPULATION

In the Upper Little Colorado, population almost tripled during the period A.D. 850–1050. This population increase terminated with population at a maximum for the prehistoric sequence in the Upper Little Colorado. Moreover, this increase was accompanied by increases in the number of sites per square mile and by a decrease in the mean distance between sites.

The increase in population and population density is understood in terms of changes in energy and integration. The population increase occurred at a time when new energy sources, upon which an expansion of population could be based, appeared. The most important of these was a new variety of corn, which was apparently better adapted to the specific environmental conditions of the arid Southwest. Tools that would allow the more efficient exploitation of the nutritional content of corn were invented or borrowed.

Additionally, a change in integrative mechanisms occurred, which had an effect on population. A central storage, perhaps redistributive, system was adopted, one that presumably afforded individuals increased protection against year-to-year variability in harvests.

DIFFERENTIATION

Changes in the structure of work were investigated at both intersite and intrasite levels. Again, significant changes were associated with the transition.

On an intersite level, the investigation focused on limited-activity sites, sites where the range of activities performed was a limited subset of the activities associated with a habitation site; 241 such sites were located, and 13 different types of sites were defined.

It was possible to show that during the transition, limited-activity sites increased in importance. The total area of such sites during the transition was high, and at some points equal to the total area of all habitation sites. Moreover, there were more different kinds of limited-activity sites present during the transition than during any other comparable period. No one type of site nor group of several types accounts for the observed variability. Finally, the location of these sites attained a maximum diversity during the transition.

Within sites, processes of differentiation were also operating. Room-to-room artifact variability was greater for Pueblo than for Basketmaker cultures. That is, rooms tended to be associated with more and more discrete sets of artifacts and activities. This trend was evident not only in the appearance of functionally specific storage rooms and ritually specific kivas, but also within the class of habitation rooms. Outdoor space on habitation sites was also utilized in more specialized fashions. Finally, there was evidence of specialization in the manufacture of some goods on the sites.

In the model, changes in differentiation were associated with changes in the dimensions of population and technology. Do the data from the Upper Little Colorado support this relationship? Increasing population and population density, which would have permitted a population large enough to afford specialization and which might also have produced resource stresses leading to conflict and to experimentation with new work arrangements, were observed. Moreover, the appearance of these new work arrangements was clearly associated with the appearance of new tools, thus, some process of mutual adaptation may be postulated.

INTEGRATION

Three data sets bearing on the integrative structures of Basketmaker and Pueblo culture were analyzed. First, the kinds of groups that inhabited settlements were characterized. Analyses by Longacre (1963) and Hill (1965) suggested that a local group in Pueblo culture was associated with about eight dwelling units. When habitation sites in the Upper Little Colorado were examined from this viewpoint, it was apparent that the transition was marked by increases in the complexity of group structures both within and between sites. There was a tendency for more and more of the local groups to inhabit given sites. At the same time, there was an observable tendency toward a regional settlement pattern in which settlements of widely varying sizes were contemporaneous.

A second effort focused on the history of the kiva, the locus of ceremonial activities in the Southwest. It was argued that the kiva developed from a pithouse that was the locus of very specific economic activities. This structure gradually acquired integrative functions. Of primary importance was the association of storage rooms with kivas during and after the transition. Three sets of data suggested this association. "Tri-wall structures," kivas surrounded by two rows of rooms that, typologically, are storage rooms appeared. Great kivas appeared with increased frequency and these sometimes had a row of peripheral storage rooms. Finally, sites with large numbers of kivas also tended to have large numbers of storage rooms. These data suggested the kiva was once the center of a redistributive system. At least, they indicated that its function was once closely tied to storing activities.

Finally, processes of role differentiation were considered through analysis of burial populations. Little differentiation was observed in Basketmaker populations, but there was good evidence for status differences in Pueblo culture. In some sites, it was possible to infer the presence of ascribed, or hereditary status.

The model suggested that changes in integration are caused by changes in the differentiation of work activities. In fact, new integrative mechanisms did begin to appear at a time when differentiation was at a maximum. As economic activities became more specialized, there was evidence for the appearance of new integrative facilities and integrative specialists who could give coherence to these increasingly diverse activities.

TECHNOLOGY

Kidder initially recorded the technological changes associated with the transition. I have tried to show that the changes that occurred did not represent simple stylistic changes, but in fact involved increasing efficiency in tool manufacture, tool use, or both. An analysis of 100 projectile points showed that the process of point manufacture in the area was simple and more efficient for Pueblo culture than for Basketmaker. An analysis of several hundred manos and metates indicated a trend toward increasing efficiency in the grinding surfaces of these tools. Finally, I noted the appearance of more developed facilities for storing food resources.

In the model, changes in technology were viewed as the result of changes in all of the other dimensions. Increasing population density necessitated new facilities for coping with larger numbers of people at a single locus. In the context of a more specialized set of activities, new tools were likely to be required and more likely to be invented. And, increasing integration reduced energy loss, which results from performing overlapping, or competing, activities.

Linking the Events

Demonstrating that a series of events occurs in contexts specified by theoretical arguments is one step in evaluating the utility of the arguments. However, it is equally important that we begin to ask whether we are dealing with a simple co-occurrence of events, or whether there is evidence suggesting that the events are causally linked. We may begin this task by looking at the event linkages in three different frameworks: the framework of temporal ordering, the framework of correlation, and the framework of systemic interaction.

Temporal Ordering

Many references to change in the anthropological literature suggest that if anthropologists had diachronic records of change, the operation of cause and effect would be clear: one variable would change, then a second, and then a third. Variables that changed early in the sequence would be interpreted either singly or cumulatively as causes of changes later in the sequence. We may evaluate this concept of cause and effect by employing data from the Upper Little Colorado, specifically, by noting when secular changes in population, differentiation, integration, and technology began, and when the *inflexion points* in the trends occurred. These data are summarized in Table 12.1 (p. 136). It must be realized that there are some problems inherent in even creating such a table. First, the figures for technology represent averages covering a number of different artifacts. Second, the figures for differentiation are based upon changes in the amount of limited-activity spaces. One would obtain slightly different estimates using a measure of the variety of such sites. I have included an energy dimension in the table based on changes in corn agriculture.

The ordering of these events is shown as a causal chain in Figure 13.1. It should be evident that the orderings based on the beginnings of the secular trend are different from those based on inflexion points. This difference is a product of a later initial change in differentiation, but a more rapid rate of change once the process is initiated. The pattern suggests that the transition began with the adoption of a new subsistence base, which was followed by a reorganization of activities in the population and the adoption of new tools appropriate to these reorganized activities. These changes, cumulatively one would assume, led to an increase in population and a subsequent reorganization of integrative mechanisms. In summary, this approach suggests that technological change should be seen as a consequence of change in some dimensions and a cause of change in others.

There is, however, a major difficulty in treating such a sequence as if it were gospel, for there were apparent fluctuations in all of the dimensions prior to and during the transition period. Such fluctuations and lags are entirely consistent with many of the statements that we make concerning the nature of human sociocultural systems.

Ordering based on points of initiation of the secular trends

Energy ⟶ Differentiation ⟶ Technology ⟶ Population ⟶ Integration

Ordering based on inflexion points

Energy ⟶ Differentiation / Technology ⟶ Population ⟶ Integration

Figure 13.1. Causal chains based on the temporal order of changes.

After all, if such systems are characterized by feedback, one would expect the initiation of any period of secular change to involve interaction and mutual feedback between critical variables. And, this interaction would in all probability show up in the form of fluctuations. The idea that the sociocultural universe is characterized by 1, 2, 3, 4 causality and the idea that it is characterized by feedback are incompatible. For this reason, simple charts of the temporal ordering of changes, while providing us with valuable information, will never satisfy our desire to understand changes. For this purpose, we need multivariate models capable of taking feedback into account.

A Statistical Approach

In order to provide a multivariate evaluation of the model, I turned to multiple correlation analysis. In the analysis, a single variable was used to represent variability in each dimension. For population, the absolute number of dwelling units per 50-year period was used. The variable used to measure differentiation was the total area of limited-activity sites per 50-year period. For integration, the percentage of dwelling units on sites with more than a single local group was employed, and for technology, a scaled measure of the increasing efficiency of tool manufacture and tool use in projectile points, manos, and metates. The primary purpose of the analysis was to evaluate the ability of the model to account for variability in technological change.

Two different analyses were run. In the first, the variables were examined for 17 50-year periods (cases) exclusive of the transition. A second analysis focused on the period of the transition itself. The square of the multiple correlation coefficient for any dependent variable represents the percentage of its variability that is explained by some system of independent variables. For the years exclusive of the transition, multiple r^2 was .79 for population; .61 for differentiation; .63 for integration; and .18 for technology. Thus, 61% of the variability in differentiation, 79% of the variability in population, 63% of the variability in integration, and 18% of the variability in technology was accounted for. During the transition, the model accounted for 72% of the variability in population, 97% of the variability in differentiation, 66% of the variability in integration, and 97% of the variability in technology. Clearly, there were important changes. Multiple r^2 for population decreased by 7%; the statistic for differentiation increased by 36%; that for integration, by 3%, and that for technology by 79%.

Two important qualifications must be made concerning this analysis. First, the coefficients are not necessarily statistically significant. For the transition, a partial correlation coefficient must be .88 or higher to be significant at the .05 level; .81 or higher to be significant at the .10 level; and .70 or higher to be significant at the .20 level. For the sequence as a whole, a coefficient must be .51 or higher to be significant at the .05 level; .44 or greater to be significant at the .10 level; and .33 or higher to be significant at the .20 level. (I do not regard a .01 or .05 level of significance as essential for accepting a correlation, especially when, as in this case, the work is highly exploratory. Significance levels provide information to work with in evaluating results; they do not confirm truth. With a risk greater than 2 chances in 10, however, I am not willing to accept the efficacy of a correlation.)

Second, only one variable was used for each dimension. Relationships between the dimension, which are exclusive of these variables, may well exist. Binford (1968a), for example, has argued that the kind of population-maintenance system that existed in a region is important in understanding the adoption of domesticates in the region. This research in no way bears on his arguments.

With these qualifications in mind, we may use the multiple and partial correlation coefficients in Table 13.1 to evaluate (1) the ability

TABLE 13.1
A Statistical Evaluation of the Model for the Sequence Exclusive of the Transition and for the Transition: Multiple Correlation Coefficients Squared and Partial Correlation Coefficients

Dependent dimension	Multiple r^2	Partial r for independent dimension			
		Population	Differentiation	Integration	Technology
For the entire sequence exclusive of the transition					
Population	.79	—	.72	.79	.13
Differentiation	.61	.72	—	−.50	.18
Integration	.63	.79	−.50	—	−.08
Technology	.18	.13	.18	−.08	—
For the transition					
Population	.73	—	.75	.58	−.69
Differentiation	.97	.75	—	−.51	.97
Integration	.66	.58	−.51	—	.62
Technology	.97	−.69	.97	.62	—

of the model to account for variability in technology and (2) the validity of postulated relationships internal to the model.

During the sequence as a whole, the model accounted for no variability at all in technological change. Nor was there a significant correlation between technological change and change in any of the model's dimensions. During the transition, however, the model accounted for 97% of the variability in technology. And, there was a significant correlation with differentiation and a nearly significant one with population. The model suggested, first, that during the transition, a primary interaction between technology and differentiation between changes in tools and changes in activities existed. It also suggested that population change may have played an important role in these changes. However, the role was not that predicted by the model—the correlation between technology and population was negative. Apparently, the adoption of technological innovations was associated with population declines rather than increases. I will attempt to deal with this anomaly later.

We may now turn to other of the predicted relationships within the model. It must be noted, however, that a partial correlation coefficient is an average of two one-way correlations. That is, it is the average of the effect of variable 1 on variable 2 and of variable 2 on variable 1. Therefore, the direction of causality must be assumed; it is not inherent in the statistics.

Changes in population were postulated primarily on the basis of changes in resources. Since, we had no adequate measure of resource change, variability in population must be left unexplained. In both the transition and the sequence as a whole, there was a significant correlation between population and integration. Such a relationship was not postulated in the model, but was evident in the data. Why? One might note that the measures of population and integration used in the analysis shared a data base—both were based upon the datum—number of rooms on a site. The correlation between the two could be a mechanical product of the shared data base. I would argue that this is not a valid argument for the question at hand. It is logically possible that integration might have increased without an increase in population. The number of rooms in the valley could have remained constant, but tended to a concentration on fewer and fewer sites. Similarly, integration could have remained constant while population increased. The total number of rooms in the valley might have grown without any increase in the number of rooms or number of local groups on a site. Therefore, I regard the positive correlation between population and integration as an important bit of information. We will consider the issue of whether changes in integration should be seen as causes of population changes, or vice versa, as we begin to reformulate the model.

We postulated that changes in differentiation would result primarily from changes in population, especially population density. During both the sequence and the transition, the correlation between population and differentiation was statistically significant. Moreover, when the variable population density was correlated with differentiation, the correlation coefficient was higher and more significant. A relationship between the energy dimension and population was also postulated. While this statistical analysis does not inform us as to the possible validity of that hypothesis, we may once again recall the apparent experimentation, the diversity in the location of limited activity loci associated with the transition.

It was argued that changes in integration would be caused by changes in differentiation. For the sequence as a whole, there was a significant correlation between the two; for the transition, there was none. Moreover, the correlation during the sequence as a whole was negative, whereas a positive correlation was posited. In other words, the immediate effect of the diversification and differentiation of the activity structure was to decrease integration. The experimentation with more kinds, and a greater quantity, of activity sites occurred when the number of local groups on a site was tending to decrease. In the model, it was postulated that the tendency to differentiation would be overcome by the adoption of new integrative strategies. The data suggested that the immediate effect of decreased integration when more different kinds of activity are being carried on—that is differentiation is increasing—is the more important. And, it was suggested that either in transitions in general or at least in the case of the Basketmaker–Pueblo transition, new integrative changes did not appear as an even response to differentiation. Instead, we are left with the earlier correlation between population and integration, and this correlation pertained only to the sequence as a whole, not to the transition. The model poorly explained changes in integration, at least for this case.

In summary, the model did adequately predict the technological changes that characterized the transition. But, apparently, some of the linkages within the model were different from those postulated. In addition, we are left in the uncomfortable position of knowing that correlations exist between the dimensions without knowing if and in what direction causality operates.

An Inferred Ordering

In Blalock's (1964) *Causal Inference in Nonexperimental Research,* he described a technique for making causal inferences from correlation matrices. Blalock reasoned that closely linked variables in a causal chain should have a higher correlation coefficient than less closely linked variables. He argued that ". . . the relationship between two distant variables should be equal to the product of intervening correlations [Pelto 1970: 30]." And, Blalock noted that if variability in any intervening variable is held constant, the correlation between the variables between which it intervenes should approach zero. If, for example, we postulated a causal chain running from population to differentiation to integration, the following conditions should be met:

1. The correlation coefficient between population and integration should be less than that between population and differentiation and that between differentiation and integration.
2. The correlation coefficient between population and integration should equal the product of the coefficients between population and differentiation and differentiation and integration.
3. If differentiation is held constant, the correlation between population and integration should approach zero.

Unfortunately, Blalock assumed that he was dealing with nonrecursive systems, that his variable systems were not characterized by feedback. Since this assumption grossly violates our assumptions about sociocultural phenomena, I will attempt to circumvent it in applying Blalock's techniques to the data at hand.

For the sequence, exclusive of the transition, the model generated when Blalock's technique is applied to the simple correlation matrix is: differentiation→population→integration. This model is inconsistent with the actual temporal ordering of events and with the model. Moreover, correlations between nonadjacent variables are too high to provide a concise fit to Blalock's criteria. Blalock would have us conclude that no causal chain is operating. I suggest that when relationships are too high for a simple linear model, we should explore the possibility that feedback is at work in the system of variables under examination. Certainly, if correlations are too low, our conclusion should be that no causal relations exist: But, when the correlations are too high, the suggestion must be that something more than a simple causal chain is being observed.

With this end in mind, we may examine a similar model derived from considering the second-order partial correlation coefficients in Table 13.1. Second-order partial correlation coefficients indicate the relationship between each pair of variables in our matrix with the other two variables held constant. We may use them to ask for each variable in the matrix with what other variable is it most highly correlated. Using this approach, we obtain the model shown in Figure 13.2. The linkages in this model are consistent with our arguments, save for the fact that the relationship between differentiation and integration is negative.

Two important observations may be made concerning the model. First, technological change is not strongly correlated with change in any other dimension. Second, the relationship between population, differentiation, and integration is a stable, negative feedback system. Given a change in any of the dimensions, following the causal sequence through the loop, the initial change will be offset after two cycles of the system. For example, population increasing implies differentiation increasing, implies integration decreasing, implies population decreasing, differentiation decreasing and integration increasing. The net result of these changes is no change.

The model properly suggested that exclusive of the transition, growth simply does not occur. Population may increase causing differentiation to increase. But a more differentiated society is, all other things being equal, less integrated. Decreasing integration means, in the case of this model, a decreased capacity for maintaining and managing the activities of large aggregates at a single locus. Population,

Technological change

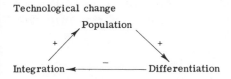

Figure 13.2. Inferred causal model for the sequence, exclusive of the transition.

therefore, declines or disperses, with concomitant effects on differentiation and integration. Technological change is unlikely to occur because, in the long run, changes in population, differentiation, and integration, which might lead to technological change, do not occur.

The application of Blalock's model to the transition period itself generates the specific model:

$$\text{population} \rightarrow \begin{array}{c} \text{differentiation} \searrow \\[0.5em] \text{integration} \rightarrow \end{array} \text{technology}$$

This model suffers from the same difficulties as that for the sequence exclusive of the transition, and we may once again attempt to remedy these difficulties by turning to second-order partial correlation coefficients. The model derived using this matrix is shown in Figure 13.3. The model corresponds to our arguments insofar as the relationships between population, differentiation, and technology are concerned. Integration is poorly tied to the remainder of the model, but its strongest link is with population, as shown. The model suggests that the technological changes that characterize the transition are a result of differentiation, which in turn is caused by population increase. Changes in integration associated with the transition appear to be more a result of attempts to manage increasing numbers of individuals than of attempts to manage increasingly differentiated activities. This is a major change in the model as first stated.

Returning to the initial model, some modifications are clearly required. First, it is apparently the case that one should not conceptualize growth as a phenomenon that can be described in a single model. The relationships among the dimensions during periods of growth are different from those that exist during periods of nongrowth. Second, if the preceding argument is correct, an investigator must be concerned with "kickers"—major changes in some variable that disrupt the underlying equilibrium of the model. Third, the effect of differentiation on integration is different from that predicted in the initial model, and this relationship must be explored further. Finally, population changes seem to have important effects on integra-

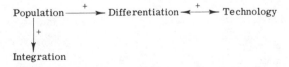

Figure 13.3. Inferred causal model for the transition.

tion that were not postulated in the model. This analysis has suggested that integrative devices in a society are first and foremost mechanisms for managing aggregates of individuals. This relationship also must be explored further.

In short, some of the arguments in the model appear, on the basis of this research, to be valid and others to be invalid. Nevertheless, an examination of the changes in the major dimensions did provide us with a means of understanding the occurrence of technological changes during the transition.

What Happened in the Upper Little Colorado?

The statistical analysis has taken us somewhat far afield from human beings and what they do. It is perhaps appropriate to attempt to translate the models into events as they may have happened in the Upper Little Colorado. Such a reconstruction was not the primary purpose of this research, and the speculative bias of the comments that I will now make must be admitted. On the other hand, it must be realized that one purpose of any piece of research is to raise new questions as well as to answer old ones.

Domesticated products were introduced into the Upper Little Colorado at about 1000 B.C. The interest of local populations in these products was apparently slight; there is no evidence for the rapid adoption of subsistence strategies based on domesticates for another 1700 years.

At about A.D. 200, there is evidence of increasing sedentism. Local populations appear to have moved into four large villages on mesa tops overlooking Hay Hollow Valley. A similar process may have been occurring throughout the Upper Little Colorado. The reasons for this shift in settlement pattern are not clear; there is no obvious association with an increased reliance on agricultural resources, although such a relationship has often been assumed in the Southwest. However, it is evident from research done in major centers of domestication that sedentism and an agricultural resource base cannot be equated. Nor is there any obvious evidence that the increasing sedentism in the area was associated with a climatic change. For the moment, we must take the appearance of a sedentary life style as a given, and note that this phenomenon merits a very detailed study at some later time.

At about A.D. 500, the abandonment of these villages began. The reasons for the abandonment are ultimately unknown, but a suggestion can be made. Different kinds of organizations are capable of managing the activities of different numbers of individuals, of organizing activities, and mediating conflicts. Archeologists often tend to assume that organizational changes occur readily in response to demographic or resource changes—in essence, every population has a ready pool of innovations that it need only dip into in order to meet some natural or social environmental contingency. This assumption is, of course, not valid. There is no reason to assume that societies in general are any less conservative organizationally than technologically. Our own experience, as well as ethnographic observations in general, suggests that societies are organizationally quite conservative. In this regard, it is important to note that there is little evidence from large pithouse village sites in the Southwest that suggests the real organizational change one might expect to accompany the appearance of large villages with large populations.

Since there is no good evidence for environmental or energetic correlates to the population dispersal, I postulate an organizational one: The villages were too large and social organization too simple to handle the complex environmental and interpersonal problems that must have existed. Local groups were caught in the trap of a population increase following sedentization, which created problems that the existing organization could not handle. Given that societies are organizationally conservative, the least-cost alternative in such a situation is dispersal.

Dispersal would, however, have had one very dire effect on the economic system of local populations. In many hunting and gathering societies, storage is essentially "on-the-hoof." A system of reciprocal relationships assures that when some member of the population acquires a perishable resource, it will be shared with other individuals in the society. Similarly, he will expect to receive similar resources when his exchange partners acquire them. A reasonably large number of individuals must reside in the same locus for a reciprocal system to be effective. Such a "critical mass" would almost certainly have been present in the four large villages. It would probably not have been present once the dispersal occurred and the population was living in what apparently were single-family sites.

Under these circumstances, it would have been necessary to find some other method of storage and a strategy of resource acquisition that could be practiced with fewer individuals in a single unit. The increased importance of storing is clearly reflected in the record of change presented in this volume, and the evidence available at the moment suggests that it was also during this period of time that the shift to agriculture began. On the one hand, agricultural plots along the valley floor could have been managed by a small organizational unit. On the other, domesticated resources do offer some advantages in storability. Nutritional evidence amassed over the last decade makes it rather clear that there would have been no perceptible, short-term nutritional advantage resulting from the adoption of domesticates. One could postulate that some advantage in the productivity per unit of land might have resulted, and such an argument would be appealing if the period in question were characterized by a large population increase. It was not, and density-based arguments do not seem appropriate in explaining the adoption of domesticates in the Upper Little Colorado. However, domesticates have advantages in storability over gathered products, a result of their hard outer tissue and the quantity of tissue that remains after drying. Moreover, acquiring a high quantity of resources from a small amount of space is just as adaptive, given limited labor inputs for subsistence resources, as it is given a large number of consumers. My suggestion is simply that the adoption of agriculture during this period may have been a product of changes in the storing needs of local populations and in the effective labor available to any consuming unit.

This new subsistence strategy did apparently prove viable. It led to a new period of increasing population. In this regard, I suggest that the adoption of an agricultural subsistence strategy, which was contingent in turn upon the population dispersal, was the kicker that initiated the process of growth in the area. The reasons for the adoption of the subsistence strategy lie in the organizational difficulties created by sedentism and in the subsequent population dispersal.

In the particular case of Hay Hollow Valley, it is important to note the outcome of the process. New organizational mechanisms that were capable of handling larger population aggregates in a single community did appear. And, the dependence on agriculture continued to increase, with the adoption of even more technological innovations—irrigation, gridding, terracing—appropriate to this activity. But, it may still be the case that the process of growth and change did not proceed far enough. For the valley and the Little Colorado were ultimately abandoned. And, the abandonment occurred during a period when a return to a heavier reliance on hunted and gathered products is in evidence. It has been assumed that this return to hunting and gathering was a temporary response to drought conditions; but, we do not know this to be the case. It could represent a return to a subsistence strategy that was more viable for the particular environmental conditions of the Southwest. The Hopi did ultimately develop an agricultural strategy appropriate to the substantial variability in rainfall characteristic of the Colorado Plateau, yet by the time they did so, most portions of the plateau had been abandoned. We must consider the possibility that the archeological record of the northern Southwest is not a record of success, but of failure. Local populations may never have developed a combination of social organization and subsistence strategies that were adaptive to local conditions.

I have identified the preceding discussion as speculation, and it should be treated as such. I offer it, however, as a testable alternative to the many hypotheses covering the adoption of domesticates now current. In our zest for ecological explanations of the origins of agriculture, we have preferred to see causal variables in the natural environment and in demographic imbalances. We have failed to give much attention to the subject that an anthropologist should be best equipped to deal with—the organizational concomitants of the adoption of domesticates. And, attention to social organization is hardly antiecological or nonecological. Nothing could be more important to the understanding of the behavior of an organism than its systematic interaction with other organisms of its own kind. Finally, I offer these speculations about the prehistory of the Upper Little Colorado as a series of suggestions concerning the kicker events which initiated the growth process.

Some Final Remarks

It is reasonable to end this work with some discussion of the limitations of the effort and with some warnings concerning the interpretations that I have made.

1.   With regard to research designs, it should be clear from this work that any research design will probably be reformulated during the course of the research. Moreover, many or some of the results that specific test implications suggest ought to be obtained will not be found. In no way does this imply that research designs are an inadequate conceptual basis for doing research. On the one hand, every piece of research has a design, and my argument is for making them explicit. On the other, a research design must be regarded

as a kind of measurement instrument—a set of arguments and suggestions as to what the world should look like given a set of assumptions and hypotheses. One formalizes these assumptions and hypotheses not in the belief that they are true, but in the belief that they deserve to be better understood. Creating a research design is setting forth a set of expectations. These expectations are the basis for "ah-hah experiences"—realizations that the world is not as the investigator thought it to be. It is such realizations that, to my mind, constitute the real source of discovery. In the absence of such a design, there is no basis for surprise, and only a limited basis for discovery. In this regard, a research design, as it is reformulated and reworked over the course of research project, is a record of discovery and learning. The fact that research designs must be reformulated is no reason for not employing them, it is one of the chief reasons to do so.

2. With regard to laws, it must be understood that the final models I have proposed in no way constitute behavioral laws. I regard them as once-tested, but still unproven, hypotheses. Moreover, it is clear that even had I firmly established the validity of these propositions, many meaningful questions would remain unanswered. I set out, for example, to evaluate the hypothesis that changes in population lead to changes in differentiation. I set forth some preliminary reasons—arguments of relevance—as to why I thought that this might be the case. If this research and other similar investigations establish that the proposition does seem to hold in a large number of cases, the confirmation of the proposition will itself imply a series of questions. Initially, one might ask why it is the case that increases in population lead to increases in differentiation. Answers to this question might be sought by evaluating some of the arguments of relevance that I presented for believing the proposition in the first place.

In the general case, the confirmation of any proposition (if x, then y) always implies at least one other question: Why if x, then y? When this question is answered—because z—another question can immediately be proposed—why if z, then if x, then y. In this fashion, one man's conclusions are always another's problems. One generation's pat answers are the questions of the next. For me, this continual process of generating new questions by answering old ones is what science is all about. True, a paradigm may specify that certain questions need not be asked. And true, an axiomatic system may define certain questions as essential and others as irrelevant, so that when the former have been answered, the latter need not be asked. But, paradigms and axiomatic systems are challenged by new generations of scientists who cannot accept the prescribed boundaries. It is fair to ask whether the arguments of relevance for the hypotheses I have tested are valid or invalid, just as I have asked whether the hypotheses are valid or invalid. This is as it should be.

3.   The definition of causality in nonexperimental research is, of course, difficult. I have employed two complementary notions of causality. On the one hand, causality is inferred from consistency between observations on the field and a set of arguments or hypotheses derived from theory and similar observations made elsewhere. On the other, it is the correlation between variables, the ability of one variable to account for variation in another. Formal arguments and substantive verification are both necessary and essential in understanding causality from this perspective. I realize that this definition is not one with which all archeologists can agree. It is, however, the one I find most appropriate to the realities of the field situation.

4.   Undoubtedly, a number of individuals will argue that my focus on factors so simple as the number of individuals in a society, the number of functioning parts of the society, and the ability of integrative mechanisms to organize human activities is overly simplified. For this simplification I do not apologize. Social scientists have succeeded in erecting a jungle of concepts that are supposed to help, but often hinder, attempts to understand behavioral and cultural variability. I think it is absolutely essential that we begin to understand better the relationship between the cultural universe and the simple characteristics of every human society that I have chosen for the focus of this research.

5.   Similarly, a number of individuals will no doubt be bothered by the lack of "ethnographic," or descriptive, content in this volume. I have, for example, said that there were different kinds of limited-activity sites, without specifying the nature of the activities conducted at each of the different kinds of sites. At the outset of the book, I gave some of my reasons for not choosing such an approach—I think that reconstruction is a difficult task and one that is not essential to understanding either change or process. It may be useful in this regard to distinguish between limited and complete inference. I have made a limited inference—the inference that activities carried on at the sites were different. I might have chosen to make a complete inference—to specify the nature of the activities carried out at each site. I did not so choose because reconstruction was not the purpose

of the research. There is no reason why an archeologist must commit himself to either limited or complete inference. He can do either, or both. In the case of the kinds of problems that I have attempted to understand in this work, it was sufficient to say that organization became more complex, sites more differentiated, population greater, etc., without specifying precisely the details of the pattern in question.

6. In only one small and highly speculative section of the work have I focused on the origin of the Basketmaker–Pueblo transition in the usual archeological sense. I have focused neither on the appearance of the first corn cob in the Upper Little Colorado, nor on the kicker which set the processes of change in motion. In the long run, it will be necessary to understand triggering events, events that apparently set processes of growth in motion. But, I feel that such an effort need not prevent us from attempting to understand processes of growth once they have begun, and this is the approach I have taken. I have constructed a model that does not assume a prime mover. Conceivably, an initial change in energy, population, differentiation, or integration could initiate the process of change in a given situation: My concern has been for what happens once that process has begun. I do not question the desirability of studying, over a series of different cases, the question of whether change in one of these dimensions is typically first. I do question the validity of assuming such events.

7. There is no doubt that many of the ideas discussed in this volume could have been made considerably more secure with more excavation data to complement the survey data that was employed. However, the collection of that additional data was not possible in the research situation. The absence of data on changing subsistence patterns is a crucial weakness of the study. Unfortunately, dry caves are unknown for the Upper Little Colorado, and the quantity and quality of such remains from open-air sites were insufficient for the task at hand. But, one cannot sit and wait for pristine testing situations without running the danger that important propositions will never be tested. I have been able to test some aspects of the model. Hopefully, other situations in which other of its aspects can be evaluated will be found.

8. A more complete evaluation of the approaches and models discussed awaits testing of the model in new situations, and with more comprehensive data sets. I am participating in one such additional test, in the Chevelon Creek drainage to the west of Hay Hollow Valley.

And, I welcome efforts by others to apply these ideas. It is my hope that such applications will be made with the intent of constructively evaluating the models—improving them by modification or replacing them with newer and better models.

Basic Survey Data

Maps of Hay Hollow Valley

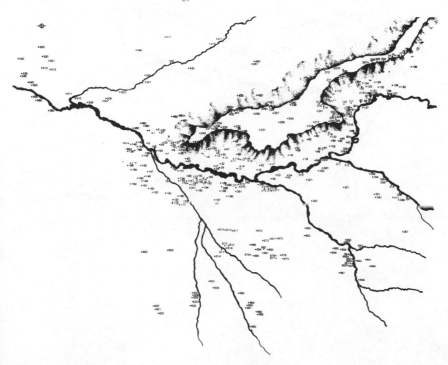

Figure A.1. Map of all sites in Hay Hollow Valley.

Figure A.2. Map of Hay Hollow Valley, A.D. 400–500.

Figure A.3. Map of Hay Hollow Valley, A.D. 600–700.

Figure A.4. Map of Hay Hollow Valley, A.D. 850–950.

168

Figure A.5. Map of Hay Hollow Valley, A.D. 1100–1200.

169

Hay Hollow Valley Sites

Site number	Date (A.D.)	Location[a]	Type[c]
1	950–1150	7	7
3	400–700	7	2
4	ND[b]	7	0
5	800–950	3	H
6	400–700	3	10
7	700–800	7	3
8	950–1150	3	H
9	1100–1200	2	3
10	950–1150	3	H
11	700–1100	3	H
12	950–1150	3	2
13	750–950	7	10
14	ND	3	0
15	700–900	3	8
16a	500–800	7	H
16b	800–1000	7	8
17	1100–1300	3	7
18	ND	7	X
19	900–1100	7	3
21	850–950	3	7
22	ND	3	0
23	950–1150	3	H
24	ND	3	X
25	950–1150	3	H
26	950–1150	3	H
27	ND	7	X
28	800–900	7	H
29	ND	7	0
30	900–1000	3	1
31	ND	2	H
33	950–1150	3	H
34	950–1150	3	6
35	ND	2	0

[a]See Chapter 10, pp. 102–103, for an explanation of type sites.
[b]ND = not datable.
[c]Location

1 = Top of Point of Mountain.
2 = Sides of Point of Mountain.
3 = Alluvial fans at base of
    Point of Mountain.

4 = Sandstone terrace tops.
5 = Lower sandstone terraces.
7 = Valley bottom Flats and Knolls.

Site number	Date (A.D.)	Location[a]	Type[c]
36	ND	2	0
37	800–900	3	1
38	ND	2	0
39	1100–1300	2	3
40	950–1150	2	1
41	950–1150	2	6
42	950–1150	2	7
43	ND	3	P
44	ND	5	P
45	700–900	2	H
46	950–1150	2	H
47	ND	2	P
48	400–700	2	6
49	950–1150	2	4
52	950–1150	3	1
53	900–1100	7	H
54	500–700	7	H
55	1000–1150	7	H
56	ND	7	X
57	950–1150	3	H
58	400–600	3	1
59	950–1150	7	H
60	950–1150	7	H
61	700–900	7	7
62	950–1150	3	8
63	950–1150	7	3
64	700–900	7	7
65	900–1000	2	H
66	900–1000	2	H
67	ND	2	P
68	950–1150	2	2
69	1350–1450	2	7
70	950–1150	2	5
71	950–1150	2	4
72	950–1150	2	5
73	950–1050	2	4
74	950–1150	2	4
75	950–1150	2	2
76	400–800	2	H
77	400–700	2	H
78	950–1150	2	4
79	950–1150	2	1
80	1000–1100	2	H
81	950–1150	2	8
83	1100–1300	7	H

Site number	Date (A.D.)	Location[a]	Type[c]
84	950–1050	7	P
85	950–1150	7	P
86	950–1150	7	10
87	950–1150	7	H
88	ND	7	0
89	650–750	7	H
90	650–750	7	2
91	550–650	7	3
92	600–800	7	H
93	700–800	7	3
94	500–700	7	H
95	500–700	7	3
96	700–900	7	H
97	850–950	7	10
98	850–1000	7	H
99	800–950	7	7
100	900–1000	7	H
102	200–500	7	X
103	950–1150	7	7
104	700–900	7	X
105	950–1150	3	H
107	ND	3	0
108	ND	3	0
109	ND	3	0
110	ND	2	X
111b	950–1150	3	8
112	950–1150	2	H
121	950–1150	3	7
122	950–1150	3	P
123	950–1150	7	H
124	950–1150	3	H
125	900–1050	6	7
126	ND	3	0
127	950–1150	7	H
128	950–1150	7	H
129	ND	3	0
130	600–700	3	2
131	400–700	3	2
132	ND	3	0
133	900–1100	7	H
134	ND	3	X
135a	500–700	3	2
135b	950–1150	3	2
135c	800–950	3	2

Site number	Date (A.D.)	Location[a]	Type[c]
136	900–1000	3	2
137	500–700	7	H
139	1000 B.C.	7	H
140	900–1000	7	H
141	900–1000	7	H
142	800–900	7	3
143	950–1000	7	3
144	950–1150	7	3
145	700–800	7	0
147	650–750	7	0
148	800–900	7	10
149	950–1150	5	H
151	ND	7	0
152	ND	7	0
153	900–1000	7	X
154	ND	7	X
155	950–1050	7	9
156	800–900	7	8
156	950–1150	7	H
157	1000–1050	7	3
158	700–800	7	H
159	800–900	7	3
160	700–800	5	3
161	900–1000	7	2
162	700–800	7	2
163	900–1000	7	10
164	ND	5	0
165	850–1000	4	2
166	900–1050	4	2
167	800–900	4	10
168	900–1000	5	10
169	500–700	5	10
170	ND	7	X
171	ND	7	X
172	550–650	7	2
174	ND	7	0
175	700–800	7	2
176	500–700	7	9
177	600–700	7	2
178	900–1000	5	5
180	800–900	7	9
181	700–900	7	3
182	950–1050	7	H
183	1000–1150	7	H

Site number	Date (A.D.)	Location[a]	Type[c]
185	600–700	7	H
186	950–1050	7	H
188	1150–1282	7	H
189	900–1000	5	H
191	900–1000	7	7
192	900–1000	7	10
193	500–700	7	10
194	700–850	7	7
195	1000–1200	7	H
196	1100–1280	7	H
197	ND	7	0
199	600–750	7	H
201	1100–1200	7	H
203	950–1150	2	7
204	950–1150	1	4
205	950–1150	1	4
206	ND	1	0
207	950–1150	1	4
208	950–1150	2	4
209	950–1150	1	4
210	950–1150	1	7
211	950–1150	1	2
212	950–1150	1	1
213	1300–1400	1	1
214	1150–1300	1	7
215	ND	2	P
216	ND	1	0
217	ND	1	0
220	ND	1	0
221	ND	1	0
222	ND	1	0
223	ND	1	0
224	ND	1	0
225	300–600	1	H
226	900–1100	1	4
227	ND	1	0
228	ND	1	X
229	1100–1200	1	6
230	ND	1	0
231	ND	1	0
232	ND	1	X
233	ND	1	0
234	1250–1350	1	4
235	ND	1	0
236	ND	1	0

Site number	Date (A.D.)	Location[a]	Type[c]
237	ND	1	0
239	700–900	1	1
240	950–1150	1	0
241	ND	1	X
242	ND	1	0
243	700–900	1	H
244	ND	2	P
270	500–700	7	H
271	850–1050	7	H
273	600–700	7	H
275	1000–1100	7	2
276	900–1000	7	2
277	900–1000	7	2
278	900–950	7	3
279	450–650	7	2
280	1000–1050	7	2
281	900–1000	7	H
282	950–1050	7	H
285	800–950	7	3
286	ND	7	X
301	1000–1100	7	X
310	950–1050	7	H
311	ND	7	0
312	950–1150	7	9
313	950–1150	7	3
314	950–1150	7	H
320	ND	4	0
321	ND	4	0
322	ND	3	X
323	ND	7	0
330	900–1000	7	2
331	950–1150	7	H
332	800–900	7	0
333	200–300	5	H
334	800–900	7	3
335	950–1150	7	3
336	800–900	7	2
337	950–1150	7	3
338	950–1150	7	7
339	950–1150	7	2
400	1000–1150	2	1
401	1000–1100	2	4
402	1000–1100	2	3
403	1000–1100	2	5
404	1000–1100	2	X

Site number	Date (A.D.)	Location[a]	Type[c]
420	1000–1150	2	7
421	1000–1150	2	H
430	1000–1150	7	H
440	1000–1150	5	1
450	1000–1100	7	H
451	1000–1100	7	H
460	ND	7	X
461	950–1050	7	H
462	1150–1200	4	H
470	1000–1100	7	7
471	1000–1100	7	2
480	ND	2	0
481	ND	2	0
482	1000–1100	3	3
490	700–950	7	H
500	850–950	7	H
501	700–800	7	H
505	900–1000	7	H
506	700–900	7	8
507	1000–1400	7	H
508	1000–1150	7	H
510	1000–1100	7	H
511	1200–1450	5	H
512	700–1000	4	H
513	ND	4	P
515	1000–1050	7	X
520	1200–1350	7	H
521	1150–1250	4	H
525	800–900	4	7
530	600–700	4	H
535	800–950	7	H
540	1000–1050	7	H
545	950–1150	7	H
550	1100–1300	7	H
555	1000–1050	7	H
560	950–1050	7	H
565	750–850	7	H
600	1000–1100	7	2
605	1000–1300	7	H
610	950–1100	7	7
611	1050–1100	7	H
612	1000–1150	7	3
613	1050–1150	7	2
614	ND	7	X
615	950–1100	7	7

Site number	Date (A.D.)	Location[a]	Type[c]
616	800–1000	7	3
617	1000–1150	7	H
620	1000–1150	7	2
621	1000–1150	7	7
622	1050–1150	7	10
630	ND	7	X
631	ND	7	X
633	950–1050	7	10
634	1000–1150	7	10
635	ND	7	X
636	1000–1150	7	2
637	1000–1100	7	2
640	ND	5	0
641	1000–1100	5	2
643	ND	5	0
644	1000–1100	5	3
645	ND	7	X
647	950–1050	5	2
649	1100–1200	5	1
650	ND	5	X
651	950–1050	7	10
652	ND	7	X
654	850–950	7	3
655	800–900	5	3
656	1000–1100	5	3
657	950–1050	7	5
658	1000–1100	5	1
659	850–900	4	8
660	ND	5	X
661	800–1000	5	H
662	200–700	5	H
663a	200–700	4	H
663b	1000–1100	4	H
670	950–1050	7	10
671	900–1050	7	3
672	1000–1100	4	H
673	1000–1150	7	H
675	950–1200	4	H
676	950–1200	4	H
677	950–1050	7	H
678	ND	7	X

Basic Site Data

Dating the Houses

Six age determinations have been obtained for the four pithouses. All of the samples used were from beams lying on the floor of the houses. Samples from Pithouses X, 1, and 2 were large chunks of wood from relatively complete beams. The sample from Pithouse Y consisted of smaller fragments.

Pithouse X was dated to A.D. 625 ± 95 by carbon-14 and A.D. 656–766 by tree-ring dating. A single carbon-14 date of A.D. 545 ± 145 was obtained for Pithouse 1. Pithouse 2 was dated to A.D. 525 ± 65 by carbon-14 and A.D. 628–726 by tree-ring. The date for Pithouse Y was A.D. 940 ± 110.

The evidence is certainly not clear cut. A date of about A.D. 700 seems appropriate for the group as a whole. However, only Pithouses 1 and 2 seem almost certainly to have been occupied contemporaneously. Pithouse X may be somewhat later, and Pithouse Y still later.

Faunal Remains

Faunal remains from the sites were analyzed at the Field Museum by Mrs. Sophie Zonas. There were no surprises. Deer and rabbit

178

accounted for most of the specimens. Prairie dog and gopher may simply have burrowed into the deposits. Rodent burrows were everywhere, and it is not inconceivable that these rodents were being consumed. Specimens of Abalone and Olivella shell were omitted from the analysis because they certainly represent trade items and not food goods.

Pithouse	Species	Count (fragments)
	Area 1	
1A/27,28CD Level 2	Rabbit (*L. californicus*)	7
1A/27,30CD	Deer (*O. virginianus*)	1
	Area X	
12B/26,27JK Level 2	Deer (*O. virginianus*)	1
12B/22,23ND Floor	Prairie Dog (*cynomys*)	1
12B/18,19BC Level 1	Deer (*O. virginianus*)	2
12B/18,19BC Level 1	Rabbit (*L. californicus*)	8
12B/20,21ND Level 1	Deer (*O. virginianus*)	1
12B/22,23PQ Floor	Gopher (*T. bottae*)	2
	Area Z	
12A/23,24ST Level 1	Rabbit (*L. californicus*)	1
12A/27,28QR Level 1	Prairie Dog (*cynomys*)	1
12A/21,22UV Level 1	Rabbit (*L. californicus*)	3
12A/25,26ST Level 1	Deer (*O. virginianus*)	1
12A/25,26UV Level 2	Gopher (*T. bottae*)	1
12A/25,26UV Level 2	Rabbit (*L. californicus*)	3
12A/27,28UV Level 1	Deer (*O. virginianus*)	2

Floral Remains

Floral remains were collected when recognized. In addition, pitfill and samples from the pithouse floors were processed by flotation. The recognized remains and the flotation samples were analyzed by Richard Hevly of Northern Arizona University.

Location	Description and Count
	Pithouse I
1A/29,30CI	*Juniperus monosperma* (1 seed)
Level 2	
1A/29,30EF	*Equisetum* (1 joint)
Floor	
1A/1,2GH	*Equisetum* (2 joints)
Floor	Corn (1 cob)
	Pithouse X
12-B/20,21NO	*Juniperus monosperma* (1 seed)
Floor	1 corn cob fragment
12-B/20,21PQ	Corn (fragments of 5 cobs)
12-B/22-23NO	*Juniperus osteosperma* (22 shaved
Floor	pierced seeds)
12-B/22,23PQ	*Juniperus monosperma* (1 seed)
Floor	
	Outside Pithouse X
12-B/22,23JK	*Cleome* (1 seed), *Cycloloma atriplicifolium*
Pitfill	(1 seed), *Leguminosea* (1 seed), *Cruciferae*
	(2 seeds), *Compositae* (Sunflower),
	(1 achene)
12-B/26,27JK	*Phaseolus* (1 seed)
Pitfill	
12-B/26,27NO	*Juniperus monosperms* (19 seeds),
	Corn (1 grain), *Juniperus osteosperma*
	(18 seeds), *Phaseolus* (1 seed)
	Area Y
14B/5,6CCDD	*Juniperus osteosperma* (1 seed)
Pitfill	
14B/5,6AABB	*Chenopodium* (1 reticulate, 1 smooth)
Pitfill	*Caryophyllaceous* or *Portulacaceous*
	(1 seed)

Pollen Analysis

Two pollen samples from the sites were analyzed by Richard H. Hevly of Northern Arizona University. The samples are washings from the surfaces of a metate (Pithouse I) and a metate fragment (Pithouse X). I hoped the analysis might show that the metate from Pithouse X was in fact used as a slab rather than as a metate. The absence of *Zea* and *Cleome* may indicate this is the case. The relatively higher percentage of pinyon might provide an indication that the cobbles and slabs were used in nutting. If this had been the case, I would have expected to find shells on the floor of the house, since carbonized juniper seed beads and corn cobs were found on the floor. None were found, and thus, the precise function is still in doubt.

The general relationship between arboreal and nonarboreal pollen corresponds with Hevly's (see earlier) previous analyses of pithouse samples from the valley.

Pollen type	Metate	Metate fragment
Pinus	17	42
Juniperus	24	22
Querous	3	2
Ephedra	5	2
Composites:		
Lo-Spine	14	15
Hi-Spine	12	10
Cheno-Am	90	89
Graminae:		
Zea	1	0
Others	34	18
Cleome	1	0
	200 grains	200 grains + fungal spores

Artifact Types

The artifact types for which counts were recorded were classified as follows:

Side Concave: A flake modified after detachment from the core so as to produce an edge on the side of the flake (relative to an axis perpendicular to the butt) that is concave and steeper than the original. Denticulate and nondenticulate types are distinguished.

Side Convex: A flake modified after detachment from the core so as to produce an edge on the side of the flake that is convex and steeper than the original edge. Denticulate and nondenticulate types are distinguished.

Side Flake: A flake modified after detachment from the core so as to produce an edge on the side of the flake that is flat and steeper than the original edge. Denticulate and nondenticulate types are distinguished.

Acute Concave: A flake modified after detachment from the core so as to produce an edge on the side of the flake that is concave and more acute than the original edge.

Acute Convex: A flake modified after detachment from the core so as to produce an edge on the side of the flake that is convex and more acute than the original edge.

Acute Flat: A flake modified after detachment from the core so as to produce an edge on the side of the flake that is flat and more acute than the original edge. Blades are distinguished.

Acute Denticulate: A flake modified after detachment from the core so as to produce an edge that is denticulated and more acute than the original edge.

Sinuous Biface: A flake modified bifacially after removal from the core so as to produce a sinuous acute edge.

End Scraper: A flake modified after detachment from the core so as to produce a steep edge at the end (relative to an axis perpendicular to the butt) of the flake.

Platform Modified: A flake whose striking platform has been significantly modified prior to, or after, detachment from the core.

Notch: A flake that has been modified after detachment from the core on a side or edge so as to produce an acute "notch" in an otherwise regular edge.

Bec: A flake that has been modified after detachment from the core so as to produce a single-pointed projection at one end of the flake.

Projectile Point: Self-explanatory.

Macrotools: Artifacts described so far have all weighed 3 ounces or less. A few flakes modified after detachment from a core weighed 6 ounces or more. Within this group, steep modifications and acute modification were distinguished.

Unutilized: A flake not modified or utilized after detachment from the core. Categories are: greater than ½ inch (counted and weighed) and less than ½ inch (weighed).

Acute Edge–Acute Wear. A flake that has been utilized after detachment from a core. The edge that has been utilized is acute, and the wear pattern is also acute. Heavily and slightly worn types are distinguished.

Acute Edge–Steep Wear. A flake that has been modified by use after detachment from a core. The edge that has been utilized is acute, but the wear pattern is steep. Heavily and slightly worn categories are distinguished.

Steep Edge–Acute Wear. A flake that has been modified after detachment from a core. The edge that has been utilized is steep; the wear pattern is acute. Heavily and slightly worn categories are distinguished.

Core. A naturally occurring piece of stone from which flakes have been detached.

Hammerstone. A stone that shows signs of having been struck continually against another object.

Manos. Used in conventional fashion.

Metates. Used in conventional fashion.

Slabs. Used in conventional fashion.

References

Adams, R.
  1966   *The evolution of urban society.* Chicago: Aldine.
Adelman, I., and C. T. Morris
  1967   *Society, politics, and economic development.* Baltimore, Maryland: Johns Hopkins Press.
Ascher, R.
  1961   Analogy in archaeological interpretation. *Southwestern Journal of Anthropology* **17**: 317–325.
Baer, W.
  1964   Regional income inequality and economic growth in Brazil. *Economic Development and Cultural Change* **12**: 268–285.
Beaglehole, P.
  1935   Census data from two Hopi villages. *American Anthropologist* **37**: 41–54.
Berelson, B., and G. A. Steiner
  1964   *Human behavior: An inventory of scientific findings.* New York: Harcourt Brace and World.
Berry, B. J. L.
  1961   Basic patterns of economic development. In *Atlas of economic development,* edited by N. Ginsburg. Chicago: Univ. of Chicgo Press. Pp. 110–119.
Binford, L. R.
  1962   Archaeology as anthropology. *American Antiquity* **28**: 217–225.
  1964   A consideration of archaeological research design. *American Antiquity* **29**: 425–441.

184

1967   Comment on Major aspects of the interrelationship of archaeology and ethnology. K. C. Chang. *Current Anthropology* **8**: 234–235.

1968a Post-Pleistocen adaptations. In *New perspectives in archeology,* edited by L. R. Binford and S. Binford. Chicago: Aldine. Pp. 314–342.

1968b Review of A guide to field methods in archaeology. Robert F. Heizer and John A. Graham. *American Anthropologist* **70**: 806–808.

Binford, L. R. and S. R. Binford

1965   A preliminary analysis of functional variability in the Mousterian of levallois facies. *American Anthropologist* **68** (Part 2): 238–295.

Bohrer, V.

1968   Paleoecology of an archeological site near Snowflake, Arizona. Unpublished Ph.D. dissertation.

Boserup, E.

1969   *The conditions of agricultural growth.* Chicago: Aldine.

Braidwood, R.

1968   Archeology: An introduction. *Encyclopedia Britannica* **2**: 225–227.

Breternitz, D. A.

1966   An appraisal of tree-ring dated pottery in the Southwest. *Anthropological papers of the University of Arizona* No. 10. Tucson: University of Arizona Press.

Brown, J. A.

1966   Dimensions of status in the burials at Spiro. Paper presented at the 65th annual meeting of the American Anthropological Association, Pittsburgh, Pennsylvania.

Burkenroad, D.

1968   Population growth and economic change. Field Museum of Natural History, Chicago. Unpublished manuscript.

Carter, G. F.

1945   Plant geography and culture history in the American Southwest. *Viking Fund Publications in Anthropology* No. 5.

Chang, K. C.

1958   Study of neolithic social grouping: examples from the New World. *American Anthropologist* **60**: 298–334.

1967a *Rethinking archaeology.* New York: Random House.

1967b Major aspects of the interrelationship of archaeology and ethnology. *Current Anthropology* **8**: 227–243.

Childe, V. G.

1951   *Man makes himself.* New York: Mentor.

Clark, C.

1967   *Population growth and land use.* New York: St. Martin's Press.

Clarke, D.

1968   *Analytical archaeology.* London: Methuen and Co. Ltd.

Coale, A. J.

1963   Population and economic development. In *The population dilemma,* edited by The American Assembly, Englewood Cliffs, New Jersey: Prentice-Hall. Pp. 46–69.

Colton, H. S.

1960   *Black sand: prehistory in northern Arizona.* Albuquerque, New Mexico: Univ. of New Mexico Press.

Connor, J.
 1968 Economic independence and social interaction: Related variables in culture change. Field Museum of Natural History, Chicago. Unpublished manuscript.
Cook, S. F., and R. F. Heizer
 1965 The quantitative approach to the relation between population and settlement size. *Reports of the University of California archaeological survey* No. 64.
Cooley, M. E. and R. Hevly
 1964 Geology and depositional environment of Laguna Salada, Apache Co., Arizona. In *Chapters in the prehistory of Eastern Arizona, II,* edited by Martin *et al.* Fieldiana: Anthropology 55.
Cutler, H.
 1952 A preliminary survey of plant remains of Tularosa cave. In *Mogollon cultural continuity and change,* edited by P. S. Martin, J. B. Rinaldo, E. Bluhm, H. Cutler, and R. Grange, Jr. Fieldiana: Anthropology 40: 461–480.
Cutler, H.
 1964 Plant remains from Carter Ranch site. In *Chapters in the prehistory of eastern Arizona, II,* edited by P. S. Martin, J. Rinaldo, E. Bluhm, H. Cutler, and R. Grange. Fieldiana: Anthropology 53: 227–234.
Dalton, G.
 1964 The development of subsistence and peasant economies in Africa. *International Social Science Journal* 16: 178–194.
Danson, E. B.
 1957 An archaeological survey of west central New Mexico and east central Arizona. *Papers of the Peabody Museum of American Archaeology and Ethnology.* Vol. 4, No. 1. Cambridge: The Museum.
Davis, K.
 1963 Population. *Scientific American* 209: 62–71.
 1968 Colin Clark and the benefits of an increase in population. Review of population growth and land use. Colin Clark. *Scientific American* 218: 132–138.
Davis, K., and J. Blake
 1956 Social structure and fertility: An analytic framework. *Economic Development and Cultural Change* 4: 211–214.
Davis, K., and H. Golden
 1954 Urbanization and the development of preindustrial areas. *Economic Development and Cultural Change* 3: 6–26.
Dean, J. S.
 1967 Aspects of Tsegi phase social organization. Unpublished manuscript.
Deetz, J.
 1965 *The dynamics of stylistic change in Arikara ceramics.* Urbana, Illinois: Univ. of Illinois Press.
Dickey, A.
 1971 Report on pollen from Hay Hollow canals. Unpublished manuscript. Field Museum of Natural History, Chicago.
Donaldson, T.
 1893 Moqui Pueblo indians of Arizona and New Mexico. *Eleventh Census of the United States, Extra Census Bulletin.* Washington, D.C.: U.S. Census Printing Office.

Durkheim, E.
  1964   *The division of labor in society.* New York: Free Press.
Eckstein, A.
  1957   Individualism and the role of the state in economic development. *Economic Development and Cultural Change* **6**: 81–87.
Eddy, F. W.
  1966   Prehistory in the Navajo Reservoir District. *Museum of New Mexico Papers in Anthropology* No. 15, Parts I and II.
Eggan, F.
  1950   *Social organization of the western Pueblos.* Chicago: Univ. of Chicago Press.
  1966   *The American Indian: Perspectives for the study of social change.* Chicago: Aldine.
Fewkes, J. W.
  1916   *Excavations and repair of Sun Temple Mesa Verde National Park.* Washington, D.C.: Government Printing Office.
Ford, R.
  1968   Jomez Cave and its place in an early horticultural settlement pattern. Paper presented to the 33rd Annual Meeting of the Society for American Archaeology, Santa Fe, New Mexico.
Frederiksen, H.
  1966   Dynamic equilibrium of economic and demographic transition. *Economic Development and Cultural Change* **14**: 316–322.
Gabel, C.
  1967   *Analysis of prehistoric economic patterns.* New York: Holt.
Gardin, J. C.
  1965a The reconstruction of an economic network of the second millennium B.C. In *The use of computers in anthropology,* edited by D. Hymes. The Hague: Mouton. Pp. 379–392.
  1965b On a possible interpretation of componential analysis in archeology. In *Formal semantic analysis,* edited by B. A. Hammel. *American Anthropologist* **67** (No. 5): 9–22.
Gellner, E.
  1964   *Thought and change.* London: Weidenfeld and Nicholson.
Gillmor, F., and L. W. Wetherill
  1953   *Traders to the Navajo.* Albuquerque, New Mexico: University of New Mexico Press.
Griffin, P. B.
  1967   A high status burial from Grasshopper Ruin, Arizona. *The Kiva* **33**: 37–53.
Hack, J. T.
  1942   The changing physical environment of the Hopi Indians of Arizona. *Papers of the Peabody Museum of American Archaeology and Ethnology* **35** No. 1. Cambridge: The Museum.
Hagen, E. E.
  1964   Personality and economic growth. In *Development and society,* edited by D. E. Nocack and R. Lekachman. New York: St. Martin's Press. Pp. 163–178.
Haggett, P.
  1966   *Locational analysis in human geography.* New York: St. Martin's Press.

Hanson, N.
  1965   *Patterns of discovery*. Cambridge: Cambridge University Press.
Harris, M.
  1968   Comments. In *New perspectives in archeology*, edited by L. R. Binford and
          S. R. Binford. Chicago: Aldine. Pp. 359–361.
Hauser, P. M.
  1964   The social, economic, and technological problems of rapid urbanization.
          In *Development and society*, edited by D. E. Nocack and R. Lekachman. New
          York: St. Martin's Press. Pp. 245–251.
Hawley, F. M.
  1950   Big kivas, little kivas and moiety houses. *Southwestern Journal of Anthropology*
          6: 286–302.
Hayes, A. C.
  1964   *The archeological survey of Wetherhill Mesa*. Washington, D.C.: National Park
          Service.
Heizer, R. F., and J. A. Graham
  1967   *A guide to field methods in archaeology*. Palo Alto, California: The National
          Press.
Hempel, C. G.
  1966   *Philosophy of natural science*. Englewood Cliffs, New Jersey: Prentice-Hall.
Hevly, R. H.
  1964   Pollen analysis of quaternary archaeological and lacustrine sediments from
          the Colorado plateau. Unpublished Ph.D. dissertation. University of Arizona.
Hill, J. K.
  1965   Broken K.: A prehistoric society in eastern Arizona. Unpublished Ph.D.
          dissertation. University of Chicago.
Hirschmann, A. D.
  1958   *The strategy of economic development*. New Haven, Connecticut: Yale Univ.
          Press.
Homans, G.
  1970   *The nature of social science*. New York: Harcourt.
Hoselitz, B. F.
  1954   A sociological approach to economic development. *Atti dei Congreso Inter-*
          nazionale di Studio sul Problema delle Aree Arretrate **2**: 765–778.
Jennings, J. D.
  1956   The American Southwest, a problem in cultural isolation. *Memoirs of the*
          Society for American Archaeology No. 11.
Johnson, J.
  1970   Settlement systems and cultural adaptation in the Hay Hollow Valley, A.D.
          950–1100. Field Museum of Natural History, Chicago. Unpublished manu-
          script.
Johnston, D. F.
  1966   An analysis of sources of information on the population of the Navajo. *Bureau*
          of American Ethnography Bulletin 197. Washington, D.C.: Government Print-
          ing Office.
Kamerschen, D. R.
  1965   An operations index of "overpopulation.." *Economic Development and Cultural*
          Change **13**: 169–187.

Kidder, A. V.
1927 Southwestern archaeological conference. *Science* **66**: 489–491.
Klieman, E.
1966 Age composition, size of households, and the interpretation of per capita income. *Economic Development and Cultural Change* **15**: 37–58.
Kluckholn, C.
1939 The place of theory in anthropological studies. *Philosophy of Science* **6**: 328–344.
Kluckholn, C., and D. Leighton
1962 *The Navaho.* Garden City, New York: Doubleday.
1967 *Mirror for man.* New York: Fawcett.
Kroeber, A. L.
1917 Zuni kin and clan. *Anthropological Papers of the American Museum of Natural History* No. 28 (Part II). New York: The American Museum.
Kuhn, T. S.
1962 *The structure of scientific revolutions.* Chicago: Univ. of Chicago Press.
Lambert, R. D.
1964 The social and psychological determinants of savings and investments in developing societies. In *Development and society,* edited by D. E. Novack and R. Lekachman. New York: St. Martin's Press. Pp. 262–277.
Lampard, E. E.
1954 The history of cities in the economically advanced areas. *Economic Development and Cultural Change* **3**: 81–137.
Lancaster, J. A.
1954 *Archaeological excavations in Mesa Verde National Park.* Washington: National Park Service.
Lausen, H.
1962 Regional income inequalities and the problem of growth in Spain. *Papers of the Regional Science Association, Europena Congress* **8**: 169–191.
Leone, M. P.
1968 Economic autonomy and social distance: archaeological evidence. Unpublished Ph.D. dissertation. University of Arizona.
Levy, M. J.
1966 *Modernization and the structure of societies.* Princeton, New Jersey: Princeton Univ. Press.
Lewin, K.
1935 *A dynamic theory of personality.* New York: McGraw-Hill.
Lister, F., and R. Lister
1968 *Earl Morris and Southwestern Archaeology.* Albuquerque, New Mexico: University of New Mexico Press.
Longacre, W. A.
1963 Archaeology as anthropology: A case study. Unpublished Ph.D. dissertation. University of Chicago.
1964 A synthesis of Upper Little Colorado prehistory, Eastern Arizona. In *Chapters in the prehistory of Eastern Arizona,* edited by Martin *et al.* Fieldiana: Anthropology 55.
1966 Changing patterns of social integration: A prehistoric example from the American Southwest. *American Anthropologist* **68**: 94–102.

Mabogunje, A. J.
  1965 Urbanization in Nigeria—a constraint on economic development. *Economic Development and Cultural Change* **13**: 413–439.
MacArthur, J., and M. Connell
  1966 *Biology of populations.* New York: Wiley.
McClelland, D. C.
  1964 The achievement motive in economic growth. In *Development and society,* edited by D. E. Novack and R. Lekachman. New York: St. Martin's Press. Pp. 179–187.
McCutcheon, M.
  1968 Population density and specialization. Field Museum of Natural History, Chicago. Unpublished manuscript.
McGregor, J.
  1965 *Southwestern archaeology.* Urbana, Illinois: Univ. of Illinois Press.
Martin, P. S.
  1929 The kiva a survival of an ancient house type. Unpublished Ph.D. dissertation. University of Chicago.
  1967 The Hay Hollow Site. *Bulletin of the Field Museum of Natural History* **38**: 6–10.
Martin, P. S., and J. B. Rinaldo
  1951 The Southwestern co-tradition. *Southwestern Journal of Anthropology* **7**: 215–229.
Martin, P. S., J. B. Rinaldo, W. A. Longacre, C. Cronin, L. G. Freeman and J. Schoenwetter
  1962 *Chapters in the prehistory of eastern Arizona, I.* Fieldiana: Anthropology 53.
Martin, P. S., J. B. Rinaldo, W. A. Longacre, L. G. Freeman, J. A. Brown, R. H. Hevly, and M. E. Cooley
  1964 *Chapters in the prehistory of eastern Arizona, II.* Fieldiana: Anthropology 55.
Merbs, C. F.
  1968 Burial patterns in the Canadian Arctic. Paper presented to the 33rd Annual Meeting of the Society for American Anthropology, Santa Fe, New Mexico.
Miller, J. G.
  1965a Living systems: Structure and process. *Behavioral Science* **10**: 337–374.
  1965b Living systems: Cross-level hypotheses. *Behavioral Science* **10**: 380–411.
Mindeleff, V.
  1891 A study of Pueblo architecture, Tusayan and Cibola. *Eighth Annual Report of the Bureau of American Ethnology, 1886–1887.* Washington, D.C.: Government Printing Office.
Myrdal, G.
  1957 *Rich lands and poor.* New York: Harper.
Naroll, R.
  1962 Floor area and settlement population. *American Antiquity* **27**: 587–589.
Nash, M.
  1958 Some social and cultural aspects of economic development. *Economic Development and Cultural Change* **7**: 137–150.
Park, R. E.
  1950 *Race and culture.* Glencoe, Illinois: The Free Press.

Parsons, E. C.
1929 The social organization of the Tewa of New Mexico. *Memoirs of the American Anthropological Association* No. 36.

Parsons, T., and N. J. Smelser
1956 *Economy and society.* New York: The Free Press.

Peckham, S.
1962 *Highway salvage archaeology* Vol. IV. Santa Fe, N.M.: New Mexico State Highway Department and Museum of New Mexico.

Pelto, P.
1970 *Anthropological research.* New York: Harper and Row.

Pepper, G.
1902 The ancient basketmakers of southeastern Utah. *American Museum Journal* **2**: No. 4.

Plog, F.
1972 Diachronic anthropology. Paper read at the 37th Annual Meeting of the Society for American Archaeology, Miami Beach, Florida.

In Press a
Explaining change. In *The explanation of organizational change,* edited by J. N. Hill. Santa Fe, New Mexico: School for American Research.

In Press b
Laws, systems of laws, and the explanation of observed variability. In *Models of culture change,* edited by C. Renfrew. London: Duckworth.

Polanyi, K.
1957 The economy as instituted process. In *Trade and markets in the early empires,* edited by K. Polanyi, C. Arensberg, and H. Pearson. Glencoe, Illinois: The Free Press. Pp. 243–269.

Polgar, S.
1964 Evolution and the ills of mankind. In *Horizons in anthropology,* edited by S. Tax. Chicago: Aldine. Pp. 200–211.

Prudden, T.
1897 An elder brother to the Cliff-Dwellers. *Harper's Magazine* **95**: 56–62.

Reals, L.
1965 A preliminary report on the County Road Site artifact distribution analysis. Field Museum of Natural History, Chicago. Unpublished manuscript.

Reed, E. K.
1964 The greater Southwest. In *Prehistoric man in the New World,* edited by J. D. Jennings and E. Norbeck. Chicago: University of Chicago Press. Pp. 175–192.

Roberts, F. H. H.
1932 The village of the Great Kivas on the Zuni Reservation, New Mexico. *Bureau of American Ethnology Bulletin III.* Washington, D.C.: Government Printing Office.

1935 A survey of Southwestern archaeology. *American Anthropologist* **37**: 44–65.

Rostow, W. W.
1960 *The stages of economic growth.* Cambridge: The University Press.

Rouse, I.
1966 Southwestern archaeology today. In *Southwestern archaeology,* edited by A. V. Kidder. New Haven, Connecticut: Yale Univ. Press. Pp. 1–55.

Rudner, R. S.
  1966 *Philosophy of social science.* Englewood Cliffs, New Jersey: Prentice-Hall.
Sahlins, M. and E. Service
  1960 *Evolution and culture.* Ann Arbor, Michigan: Univ. of Michigan Press.
Saxe, A. A.
  1968 Explaining variability in disposal of the dead: social relationship factors. Paper presented to the 41st annual Pecos Conference, El Paso, Texas.
Schoenwetter, J. and A. Dittert
  1968 An ecological interpretation of Anasazi settlement patterns. In *Anthropological archaeology of the Americas,* edited by B. Meggars. Washington, D.C.: Anthropological Society of Washington. Pp. 41–66.
Schroeder, A.
  1965 Unregulated diffusion from Mexico into the Southwest prior to A.D. 700. *American Antiquity* **30**: 297–309.
Schwartz, D.
  1956 Demographic changes in the early periods of Cohonina Prehistory. In *Prehistoric settlement patterns,* edited by G. Willey. *Viking Fund Publications in Anthropology* No. 23.
Shils, E.
  1964 The military in the political development of the new states. In *Development and society,* edited by D. E. Novack and R. Lekachman. New York: St. Martin's Press. Pp. 392–405.
Sigerist, H. E.
  1943 *Civilization and disease.* Ithaca, New York: Cornell Univ. Press.
Smelser, N. J.
  1963 *The sociology of economic life.* Englewood Cliffs, New Jersey: Prentice-Hall.
Spaulding, A. C.
  1953 Review of Measurement of some prehistoric design developments in the southeastern states. James A. Ford. *American Anthropologist* **55**: 588–591.
  1968 Explanation in archeology. In *New Perspectives in archeology,* edited by L. R. Binford and S. R. Binford. Chicago: Aldine. Pp. 33–40.
Spengler, J. H.
  1961 Population change: Cause, effect, indicator. *Economic Development and Cultural Change* **9**: 249–266.
Steward, J. H.
  1937 Ecological aspects of Southwestern society. *Anthropos* **32**: 87–104.
  1955 *Theory of culture change.* Urbana, Illinois: Univ. of Illinois Press.
Stewart, J. Q., and W. A. Warntz
  1967 The physics of population distribution. In *Spatial analysis,* edited by B. J. L. Berry and D. F. Marble. Englewood Cliffs, New Jersey: Prentice-Hall. Pp. 124–141.
Straus, L. G.
  1968 Social stratification in pithouse villages. Field Museum of Natural History, Chicago. Unpublished manuscript.
Titiev, M.
  1944 Old Oraibi, a study of the Hopi Indians of Third Mesa. *Papers of the Peabody Museum of American Archaeology and Ethnology* No. 22. Cambridge: The Museum.

Toffler, A.
1970 *Future shock.* New York: Random House.
Traugott, J.
1968 The isolation and measurement of stylistic variation. Field Museum of Natural History, Chicago. Unpublished manuscript.
Tumin, M. M.
1964 Competing status systems. In *Development and society,* edited by D. E. Novack and R. Lekachman. New York: St. Martin's Press. Pp. 222–232.
Turner, C. G. and L. Lofgren
1966 Household size of prehistoric Western Pueblo Indians. *Southwestern Journal of Anthropology* **22**: 117–132.
Vivian, G.
1959 *The Hubbard Site and other tri-wall structures.* Washington: National Park Service.
Vivian, G. and T. W. Mathews
1964 Kin Kletso. *Southwestern Monuments Association Technical Series* No. 6. Globe.
Vivian, G. and P. Reiter
1960 The great kivas of Chaco Canyon. Santa Fe, New Mexico: School of American Research No. 22.
Wendorf, F.
1956 Some distributions of settlement patterns in the Pueblo Southwest. In *Prehistoric settlement patterns in the New World,* edited by G. Willey. *Viking Fund Publications in Anthropology* No. 23.
Whallon, R.
1965 The Owasco period: A reanalysis. Unpublished Ph.D. dissertation. University of Chicago.
Wheat, J. B.
1955 Mogollon culture prior to A.D. 1000. Memoir of the American Anthropological Association No. 82. American Anthropological Association, Washington, D.C.
Wheeler, M.
1956 *Archaeology from the earth.* Baltimore, Maryland: Pelican.
White, L.
1959 *The evolution of culture.* New York: McGraw-Hill.
Willey, G. and P. Philips
1958 *Method and theory in American archaeology.* Chicago: Univ. of Chicago Press.
Wynne-Edwards, V.
1962 *Animal dispersion in relation to social behavior.* Edinburgh: Oliver and Boyd.
Young, F. and I. Fujimoto
1965 Social differentiation in Latin American Communities. *Economic Development and Cultural Change* **3**: 344–352.
Zilen, J.
1968 Storage: An environmental stabilizing device. Unpublished manuscript. Field Museum of Natural History, Chicago.
Zubrow, E.
1971a Unpublished Ph.D. dissertation. University of Arizona.
1971b Carrying capacity and dynamic equilibrium in the prehistoric Southwest. *American Antiquity* **36**: 127–138.

Index